# Motivating Your Money

## A Road Map to Long-Term Wealth Accumulation

M. Russell Giveans, PhD

ISBN:1500946133
ISBN-13:9781500946135

# DEDICATION

This book is dedicated to my amazing wife Amber. She is the love of my life, the mother of my wonderful children and my best friend.

# ACKNOWLEDGMENTS

I would like to publically acknowledge the following individuals for their contributions to the editing of this book: Amber Giveans, Randy Giveans (MBA, Corporate Financial Analyst), and my CPA team. Their hard work, support and advice have been invaluable!

# TABLE OF CONTENTS

"Wisdom is even better when you have money. Both are a benefit as you go through life." – King Solomon

Ecclesiastes 7:11 (New Living Translation of the Bible)

# PREFACE

When it comes to the world of personal finance, there is no shortage of information available for the average American to obtain. From investing to budgeting, from mutual funds to bonds, and from life insurance to wills, there are many in-depth books out there that will teach you everything you need to know about your finances.

However, in my opinion, there is a major flaw in the majority of these resources: they are actually *too* in-depth! If we are totally honest about it, most will agree that 95% of Americans will not pick up a 300-page book of any kind, let alone one on the topic of personal finance! The problem with this mentality is that there are dozens of 300-page books that are absolutely vital to one's success in almost every area of life that we should be reading. Because whether you believe it or not, the saying "knowledge is power" will always hold true. And in today's culture, we fail to realize the vast amount of powerful knowledge that we forfeit by simply not taking the time to acquire it.

In my own professional life, scientific articles (published in national and international journals) are the number one way to share in-depth knowledge on a particular subject to the community. These publications are peer-reviewed and generally range from 5 – 20 pages in length. At the beginning of each journal article, the author reviews all relevant information from previously published articles on similar topics. This information is then condensed into a handful of sentences or paragraphs and enables the reader to better understand the topic at hand. In essence, this "introduction" section gives the reader a foundational knowledge about the topic being researched, and for many this serves as a "refresher course" on information that, on some level, they have already obtained. This concept of combing a wide range of knowledge into one concise resource is the basis on which I wrote this book.

Another flaw I have found with personal finance books is that they are mostly written by accountants, financial advisors and professional investors. I have nothing against these individuals, but they, like many other professionals, often write their books on such a level that only their colleagues are able to understand. Again, these books are very valuable in training and educating a certain group of individuals that need to have this level of understanding, but for the overwhelming majority of Americans, 300 pages on the same topic is nothing short of excessive to the point of frustration.

There are many topics that are essential for achieving success when it comes to one's personal finances, but it has been shown that, in the majority of Americans, a mere foundational knowledge of each of these topics is severely lacking. This is not mentioned to be a criticism, but rather a statement of fact! This has resulted in a generation of individuals who have very little confidence in their ability to succeed financially.

Finally, if you want a glimpse of the financial power you may have been forfeiting through your lack of knowledge when it comes to personal finances, then take a quick peek at the table in Appendix A (pages 138-142). This shows you what can be obtained with an investment of as little as $150 per month over the course of your life. The beauty of this table is that is works regardless of the amount of money you make on an annual basis!

If you learn the principles laid out in this book, you will see that anyone, and I mean that quite literally, can motivate their money to do exactly what *they* tell it to do, and ultimately become "financially free" by the time they reach retirement!

Don't believe me? Then keep flipping the pages and you will see for yourself!

# PART I – Fundamentals of Wealth Building

## CHAPTER 1 - INTRODUCTION TO PERSONAL FINANCE

When hearing the word "motivation," most Americans think of it in terms of succeeding in life, losing weight or becoming a better person. Rarely do we associate the term motivation with personal finance. However, I would argue that an individual's financial game plan is the area that needs the *most* motivation!

When researching the topic of personal finance, I have found that there are no fewer than 100 books on the market today, many of which the financial experts of the world would consider "must reads." Well, if the so-called experts in the world of finance are labeling these books as "must read," then why are such a small fraction of Americans actually reading them? This is why I have set out to write a clear, concise and practical book that educates the reader on creating a life-long, wealth-building strategy that anyone can follow, regardless of your age or annual income! This applies whether you are young or old, or in the bottom 1% or the top 1% of income earners. If you successfully apply the basic principles that you read throughout this book, then you will achieve a level of financial freedom that you may not have ever dreamed was possible. Conversely, if you fail to apply these basic principles to your financial life, then you will likely end up having worked hard for decades with little or nothing to show for it.

At its core, this book is about educating the reader on practical topics such as saving, spending and investing for long-term wealth accumulation. When applied correctly and consistently, this knowledge will bring financial harmony to your home on a monthly basis, affording you the freedom to live comfortably throughout your working years, and ultimately lead you into a prosperous retirement!

In my extensive research, I have found that the two primary reasons why people fail in the area of finances are 1) a lack of understanding, and 2) a lack of application. For that matter, it is almost universally true that the reason we fail in any area of life is due to a lack of understanding and application. Without each other, success is simply not attainable. No matter how much you know about a subject, if you do not apply the principles correctly and consistently, then you will not achieve the desired level of success. As you read through this book, you will certainly be given ample opportunity to receive the level of understanding required for financial success. I can only hope that, along with this knowledge, you will also be encouraged to *apply* these principles to your life! After all, knowledge and understanding without action will get you absolutely nowhere in life! And that's a guarantee!

In terms of the importance of acquiring knowledge, there is a Biblical proverb that says "In all your getting, get understanding." There is life-changing wisdom in that simple quote. It amazes me that in America today, people are constantly striving to get, get, get. They want to get fame, power, money, respect, material goods and more, yet they seem to ignore the fact that it takes a substantial amount of knowledge and understanding in order to successfully acquire any of these. I will end this topic with a quote by Dr. Creflo Dollar that I fully adhere to and whole-heartedly believe: "Your success in any area of life is based entirely on what you know about it."

When dealing with long-term wealth accumulation and retirement, it is important to understand the reasons why saving and investing are very often neglected until it is too late. When it comes to accumulating the resources (i.e. money) needed to successfully navigate through life and to have a luxurious and comfortable retirement, the following three mindsets are experienced by millions of Americans, and almost 100% of the time they lead to disastrous outcomes:

1) I'm in my 20s, why in the world would I be thinking about long-term wealth accumulation (i.e. retirement) when I just started my career?! I'm finally out on my own and making some money, so I deserve to be able to spend it however and whenever I choose!

2) I make a pretty decent salary, especially compared to when I was in my 20s. Now that I'm in my 30s, I enjoy being able to buy more expensive things and go on nicer vacations than I did before. I have plenty of time before I have to worry about retiring. I'll just throw some money in my savings account or 401(k) whenever it is convenient.

3) I'm already in my 40s or 50s, and every television show I see or website I read tells me how important it is to start saving and investing early so that my money can grow over the next 30 or 40 years. Unfortunately, now I'm too old and I don't have enough time for my money to grow if invested. I'll just keep working hard and save some extra money when I can. My savings and social security will take care of me when I cannot work anymore.

Here is the interesting thing about these three mindsets described above: if you believe mindset #1 when you are young, you are much more likely to adopt mindset #2 as you grow older. Similarly, if you have mindset #2 in your 30s, then you are again much more likely to end up with mindset #3 in your later years. When this cycle runs its course, you will likely find yourself at 60 years old, having very little to no wealth accumulation, and having to financially struggle through life in your 70s and beyond.

I do not say any of this to scare you, but rather to point out to you the importance of having a plan, sticking to it and being consistent, regardless of your current age. If you are 21 years old and just starting your career, or if you are 55 years old and have seemingly no hope for a wealthy retirement, let me share with you a simple, two-word saying that is guaranteed to improve your financial situation:

START TODAY!!!

Like I said earlier, this book is intended to be a concise and comprehensive (yet not overly detailed) overview of everything an individual should know about personal finance and investing. The ideal age range that this book is geared to is 15 - 55 years old. Why this range? Well, I assume that 15 years old is the youngest age in which a person will start his or her working career (obviously this number will vary on an individual basis). Furthermore, if you are able to grasp and take to heart the information in this book while you are in high school or college, there is almost a 100% chance that you will become a MULTI-millionaire by the time you reach your 60s.

As for age 55, I use this because it is the age at which you still have the potential for 15-20 years of investment growth before retirement. Of course if you are just starting to apply these principles at age 55, you are very much "behind the proverbial 8-ball," but it is certainly not impossible to turn things around and still achieve a comfortable and successful retirement.

Now what about those people who are over 55? Well, the fundamental principles in this book will still apply and should be adopted if they have not already been a regular part of your financial lifestyle up to this point. The only caveat would be the lack of time available for your investment portfolio to grow and not be affected by the short-term rises and falls that any investment may experience. Even so, the saying still holds true that it is "never too late" to start getting your personal finances whipped into shape, so I would absolutely recommend that you use this book to help control your financial future!

Although the fact of the matter remains that the younger you are, the greater the impact that wise financial decisions (saving, investing, etc.) will have on your long-term wealth accumulation, please do not be discouraged if you are reading this book later in life! If you are in your 50s or 60s and have not been wise with money for the past several decades, then yes, you will have to accept the fact that your "nest egg" will be substantially smaller than the numbers that I use throughout this book. However, no matter what your age is today, I can assure you that applying the principles discussed in this book will enhance your financial future by a substantial amount!

In addition, I would also like to state that there is essentially no amount of monthly income that prevents you from benefiting from the principles found in this book. Even if you are making upwards of $50,000 *per month*, in order to achieve the level of financial success that ensures a retirement lifestyle equivalent to what you desire, you must adhere to the basic principles of wealth accumulation (i.e. living on less than you make, saving, investing, etc.).

One final thought: My goal here is to motivate you to start taking control of your money habits, and thus transform your life for years to come, as well as for generations to come! Once you realize that you can, in fact, be in control of your money as opposed to the other way around, then it will empower you to start making wise financial decisions that will impact almost every area of your life! This, of course, includes being able to fulfill many of the desires you have for your life (and the lives of those around you) that have always been hindered by a lack of financial freedom. Now that's something to get excited about!

# CHAPTER 2 – HOW DO I BEGIN?

Now that you have decided to take control of your financial future, the biggest question is "how do I begin?" Before we start, let me just congratulate you for making the conscious decision to change your financial future forever, and let me also warn you that this is going to be challenging, exciting and an empowering process, all wrapped up into one! If you are up for the challenge, and are ready to be committed 100% in spite of any circumstances surrounding you (including what other people may think), then this book may very well change your life!

Okay, let's begin!

Have you ever asked yourself this question: "Where is all of my money going every month?" If you have, then consider yourself normal! The vast majority of Americans have not only asked themselves this question, but continue to ask it month after month. Why? Because they have never taken the time to sit down and learn how to "motivate their money" so that it will do what they want it to do!

Now in order to learn how to do this, we need to first discuss what many refer to as the "Bucket Analogy." For the vast majority of working individuals, your money is distributed into (or flows through) four buckets: Income Bucket, Expenses Bucket, Asset Bucket and Liability Bucket. Let's break these down, starting with the first two.

Initially, your "Income Bucket" will be your largest bucket, as it is where all of your income enters (i.e. paycheck, compensation, salary, etc.). Out of your "Income Bucket" flows a specific monthly amount into your "Expenses Bucket." This contains everything that you are obligated to pay on a monthly basis (i.e. mortgage, rent, utilities, insurance, gas, food, credit card payments, car payments, other debt, etc.).

From here, you become one of two types of people: Type 1 - those that HAVE money remaining in their "Income Bucket" after filling their "Expenses Bucket," or Type 2 - those that DO NOT HAVE money remaining after filling their "Expenses Bucket."

Let's put it in different terms. Those that spend LESS than they make (or live below their means), are the ones we will call Type 1. Those that spend MORE than they make (or live beyond their means) are the ones we will call Type 2. This is pretty straightforward, right?

One of the primary goals of this book is to motivate your money in such a manner that it does not ALL leave the "Income Bucket" and end up in the "Expenses Bucket." Of course this is much easier said than done. It is just like saying "burn more calories than you take in on a daily basis, and then you will lose weight." Again, this is easier said than done, and this is precisely why our money (as well as our bodies) needs continual motivation in order to succeed.

So I think it is safe to say that the first goal for each of us should be to live our lives as Type 1 individuals as opposed to Type 2. The indisputable fact of the matter is that you will NOT live a financially prosperous life if your monthly expenses equal or exceed your total monthly income (i.e. if you have nothing left at the end of the month).

If you are currently a Type 1 person, making more money than you spend each month, then you will likely have a decent understanding of the concepts discussed on the following pages. Even so, there are probably some areas that still have room for improvement.

If you find that you are Type 2 (having no money remaining in the "Income Bucket" once the "Expenses Bucket" has been filled), then there are basically only two ways to change your circumstance. The first option is to increase your monthly income, and the second option (which is often easier) is to decrease your monthly expenses. Each option requires quite a bit of elaboration, so let's dig deeper.

INCREASING YOUR INCOME

In order to increase your monthly income, there are several variables that come into play. Only you know your specific situation, so some of these suggestions may not entirely apply to you.

1) Increase your hourly rate

This is clearly one of the most obvious suggestions. The real question though is "how?" The first way to go about doing this is to professionally ask your boss or superior to consider offering you a raise. Depending on how long you have worked at your current job, and/or your level of productivity, this may or may not be an easy solution. At the very least, and if you do not already have the answer in writing, you can simply ask if and when a raise would be considered based upon the specifics of your situation/job classification.

Another basic solution for increasing your income is so easy that it almost sounds insulting (so please do not take it that way!). I recently heard a true story of a man in his late twenties who said that within the past year his salary had doubled. When asked to elaborate on how he obtained this incredible pay increase, he answered very matter-of-factly. He simply said, "I felt I was worth twice what my current company was paying me, so for the next 3 months I decided to go out and apply for as many jobs as I could that were offering twice the salary that I was making. I did this until I was offered one of those jobs." Voila! Talk about an incredible return on his investment of time and effort! I realize that this is an isolated case, but I also wonder how many of these stories never come to fruition because the person never takes the time to fill out the application in the first place due to fear of failure.

2) Increase the number of hours that you work each week

Again, this seems to be a very basic idea, but this one is actually far more attainable than you think. When this suggestion comes up, most people think that it is referring to their current job. While it would be ideal to simply be given the opportunity to expand your current job hours, this may not be an option. However, picking up a flexible, part-time job is a very realistic possibility. Finding a warehouse job, delivery job or weekend job is a lot more doable than you think. In fact, depending on your personal skills (experience, licensure, etc.), there may be several jobs out there looking for someone on an as-needed basis that could help increase your income.

3) Enhance your training/education

This may be the most difficult due to the fact that you will have to commit personal time and finances to take classes or attend training, but this also may be the most lucrative. Depending on your current situation (married, single, children, etc.), you may be able to finish that degree you started, or re-direct your future with a different career path, and in the process increase your income by 10%, 50% or even 100%. At the very least this should be seriously considered as a viable option.

Of course there are many other ways to increase your monthly income (spouse goes back to work, start your own business, etc.), but if the income side of the equation is truly where the problem lies, then something must be done to address this, and now is the time to do it!

## DECREASING YOUR EXPENSES

Now what about those people whose primary problem is that their "Expenses Bucket" is too large? I'm glad you asked! Reducing expenses is infinitely easier than increasing your income, in theory. However, putting into practice these changes may seem nearly impossible! This is where the true "hard work" comes into play: making the mental decision to make the change!

If you were to look at all of your monthly expenses written down line by line, how many of these would you consider "essential" for your daily living? I know some of you would say that your morning visit to the coffee shop is absolutely "essential," but let's take a minute to really look at it with an unbiased eye. If increasing your income is simply not a possibility (and just for the record, that statement is *almost* never true), then the only option that remains is to decrease your spending habits. In his book "The Automatic Millionaire," of which I highly recommend, author David Kahn coins the phrase "latte factor." He explains that for nearly every person that he has advised over the years, there is some regular and often small expense, that when added up over the course of a month, amounts to a fairly significant total. For example, a person who spends $4.00 on a latte every weekday is essentially spending $80 a month ($4.00 x 5 days x 4 weeks). This same person often says that they have no money to invest each month. Well, over the course of a year that person could be using their latte money to invest/save almost $1,000! There are also likely to be several other items that could be eliminated or greatly reduced to add even more to that total.

I realize that decreasing your expenses is not always as simple as giving up coffee. Sometimes it means cutting off the cable television, or eating out only once per week instead of three times (or dare I say zero times a week!). Whatever it entails for your situation, it is essential that you make the conscious decision to enforce a change for the betterment of your financial future, because as we stated earlier, you cannot prosper financially if you are "spending" all of your money that comes in every month.

Let me leave you with one more thought on this topic. As we will explain in later chapters on saving and investing, one of the underlying principles at play in the lives of people who spend all of their money before the end of the month is this: they simply do not know how to value their money. What I mean by this is that they see a dollar and equate it to what it can buy them right now for their own pleasure. For example, an extra $100 in their hand is seen as a new pair of shoes, a fancy dinner downtown or tickets to a sporting event. With this book, I would like to not only challenge this way of thinking, but turn it upside down! One tried and true way to decrease your expenses and motivate your money is to radically change your perception regarding the value of a dollar. Instead of seeing $100 in terms of what it can buy you *now*, I would like to propose to you the idea of seeing it in terms of what it can do for you in the future. If it is merely saved, then what it instantly becomes is a $100 safety net for when financial emergencies arise in your future (and they will...over and over again!). If it is invested wisely, then it compounds or grows over time to produce many multiples of itself that can provide stability and security for when you are no longer working for an income (i.e. retirement). If we can start to value money in terms of its future worth, then more than likely we will instantly change our current spending habits for the sake of our future!

Before we move on to discussing the different strategies for limiting your expenses and making sure that there is additional money each month, let's first briefly discuss the remaining two buckets: "Liability Bucket" and "Asset Bucket."

If you find yourself with additional money each month after the "Expenses Bucket" has been filled, there are basically two options on how you can use that money. You can either put that money into liabilities or into assets. Liabilities are simply defined as anything that does not add to your overall wealth. Examples would be jewelry, electronics, clothcs/shoes (beyond the necessities), vacations, vehicles (motorcycle, ATV, boat, etc.) or anything else that could be categorized as "stuff." All of these items likely go down in value over time, and thus are really only purchased for their present value.

Assets, on the other hand, are defined as anything that adds to your overall wealth. Examples would be investments, savings, businesses, rental real estate, etc. These items are all purchased for their long-term appreciation (increase) in value, and will ideally one day pay you back several times over!

Let me pause here and be very clear on something. I am NOT saying that liabilities should never be purchased! Many, if not all, of the items considered liabilities bring enjoyment to our lives and can be a very wonderful use of our money. My wife very much enjoys when I purchase "liabilities" for her, and I enjoy them as well (especially the vacation category!). However, it is imperative that you understand the true "cost" of purchasing these items. If liabilities are purchased at the sacrifice of acquiring assets, then you have grossly over-valued these items and have severely compromised your potential for long-term wealth accumulation.

I am not saying that the following point-of-view must be shared by everyone that reads this book, but it sure wouldn't hurt if it was! I am currently at the point in my life where it is absolutely required that in order to purchase any *substantial* liability, I must first have acquired an equal or greater amount of assets. In other words, every year I use more of my money acquiring assets than I do purchasing liabilities. If my wife or I desire a certain item (accessory, piece of jewelry, vacation, etc.), then we first make it a priority to have invested that same amount before any purchases are made. Whether this amount is $100 or $1,000, this system really makes us think twice about how much we want that liability. This is a sure-fire way to help us keep our money values in line with our long-term wealth accumulation goals.

The more you start to prioritize the acquisition of assets, the more your frivolous spending on liabilities will diminish. This paradigm shift in and of itself will have a dramatic effect on your personal wealth building potential. And as your "Asset Bucket" continues to grow, an amazing transformation will one day take place…instead of spending money from your "Income Bucket," you will find that you have the ability to spend money from your "Asset Bucket" to fund the purchase of your liabilities. The thought of this is so foreign to the vast majority of Americans that it just simply does not make sense. With the wisdom and advice that I will be sharing with you throughout this book, you can and will be in the position one day to not have to "earn" money in order to spend it. Instead, the resources that have been accumulated within your "Asset Bucket" will be able to provide you all of the money that you need, and thus be the avenue through which your future expenses are paid!

Before we get too far into how to accumulate assets (which will be explained in later chapters), there are a few more things we need to discuss in order to keep your expenses in line so that you can have surplus at the end of every month.

# CHAPTER 3 - DEBT

Now beyond the reduction of simple, everyday expenses, there is one other major area that needs to be discussed: and that is the "four-letter word"...DEBT.

Americans in today's culture have a very skewed perception when it comes to the consumption of goods (or in more modern vernacular: "buying stuff"). We live by the widely accepted, yet fatally flawed, mindset of "if I can afford the monthly payment, then I can buy it."

"What's wrong with that mindset?" you may be asking. "Where should I begin?" is my response!

Americans learn at a very young age (high school, if not before), that in order to be and feel successful, that you must look successful. So how does this play out? Here is a story of the average college graduate, from a financial perspective (using national averages):

At 23 years old, John Doe graduates with an undergraduate degree and $35,200 in student loans. Depending on the "payback plan" he opts for, his monthly payment will be $250-$500 per month. Of course now he needs a car, and assuming he makes a somewhat wise decision to buy a used car, his monthly payment for that will be $351 (if he buys a new car, his monthly payment will be $452). He now finds himself making a legitimate paycheck compared to what he had been making with his part-time, on-campus job. His friends are all making decent money now as well, so the only logical thing to do in his mind is to start enjoying his hard earned money. As his friends start buying outfits, jewelry, electronics, vacations, etc., he does the same thing so that he doesn't feel "left out." And how does he decide what he can and cannot afford? Well, he first looks in his checking account and spends that money, and then he puts the rest on his wonderful credit card, making sure all the while he can afford the minimum payment. Before he knows it, he has racked up $15,950 in credit card debt, and finds himself with a minimum payment of over $300 per month.

This little scenario may sound extreme, but it is merely using national averages to paint the picture of what many Americans are either currently facing, or will be facing if they do not take control of their finances at an early age. In this example, John Doe has a monthly minimum debt payment of nearly $1,000. The baffling part of this statistic is that if he is making a decent salary of $40,000 per year (with his monthly, after-taxes, take-home pay being roughly $2,500 per month), his debt payments are eating away about 40% of his income!

Think about that. We haven't even talked about where John Doe is going to live. In this case, he will be forced to rent something in the $500-$750 per month range, or living back at home. Further, he will have practically nothing left over at the end of each month to save and invest. In summary, this is clearly not the formula for long-term financial success!

Okay, with all of that said, you are likely to be in one of three groups: 1) someone that has never amassed much debt of any kind (except maybe a home mortgage), therefore this information does not really apply to you, 2) someone that finds themselves in a similar situation to our John Doe example, and would like to know what you should do, now that you have acquired debt, or 3) a young person who is just beginning your career, and you want to know what the solution is for not ending up with debt like the average American.

# GROUP 1

If you are in Group 1, congratulations! You have done a fabulous job in this arena, and although you may not directly benefit from it, I encourage you to read the sections on Groups 2 and 3. They will likely provide you with information on what to say to a friend or loved one that happens to be in one of those groups. The next stop for you is learning all about saving, investing and long-term wealth accumulation!

# GROUP 2

If you are in group 2, let me congratulate you for taking the step to pick up this book and for making the decision to start motivating your money! It is never too late, and if you are willing to do whatever it takes, then you will break free from your current financial situation and be on your way to building great wealth!

Before going any further, I highly recommend that everyone reads the book entitled "The Total Money Makeover" by Dave Ramsey. What he explains in detail in his book, I will briefly cover here, as I agree with most (if not all) of his guiding principles.

The first step you need to take in freeing yourself from your current financial turmoil is to build up a small cash reserve. This should be roughly $1,000-$2,000 (use the higher end if you are married and/or have children). This will eventually be the foundation for your "emergency fund," which we will address shortly. The purpose of this account is two-fold: to give you confidence that you can in fact win with money, and also to give you a cushion to take care of any unforeseen expenses while you are eliminating your debt. For some of you, saving this dollar amount may seem like a very difficult endeavor. Let me offer you two pieces of advice to combat this doubt. First, every additional $100 that you save will very likely build up your motivation for conquering this challenge. Second, if you are a little weak on the self-control side of things, then this small savings account should NOT be linked to your checking account, and better yet, it should not even be with the same banking institution! I would recommend a high-interest savings account or money market account. Make sure you are putting this into a "safe" savings account, but remember, this is not a "money-making" account, it is simply for emergencies. Once you have completed this step (and this may take selling a few things or saving every single dollar that you possible can), then you are ready to take on your debt.

The best strategy for eliminating your debt is to list each one of them (not including your home mortgage if you have one), from smallest to largest. From here, you make the absolute minimum payments on each debt. For your smallest debt however, you take any extra money you have and pay it towards this debt. After a while (depending on the size of the debt), the smallest debt will be paid off. You then take all of the money that you were applying to that first debt, and apply it to the minimum payment that you are making on your second smallest debt. With the extra money going towards this debt, it too will be eliminated more quickly than you anticipated. You continue to do this process (referred to as the "debt snowball" by Dave Ramsey) until all of your debts are paid. Please understand that this process could take up to several years (if not more), depending on how much debt you have. Once you have eliminated all of your debt (other than your home), you are ready to move on to the next step.

Do you remember that small emergency fund that you saved initially? Well, this now needs to become a full-fledged emergency fund. What this means is that you should save (as fast you can) at least 25% of your annual gross income or roughly 6 months of your household expenses. In other words, if you make $40,000 a year, then your emergency fund should be at least $10,000. In terms of 6 months of expenses, if you can operate your household budget on $2,000 a month, then your emergency fund should be about

$12,000. As a reminder, this is an emergency fund, which means it should not be touched or even looked at unless you have an emergency that you cannot pay for with your normal monthly income. And by the way, I can almost guarantee that this emergency fund will actually help you sleep better each night!

Now that you are out of debt and your emergency fund is at least 25% of your income or 6 months' worth of expenses, you are now ready to start investing for long-term wealth accumulation, or as some may call it: "Retirement."

**NOTE:** There are two scenarios where the process above should be amended:

1) If it is going to take you longer than 5 years to eliminate all of your debt (other than your home)

2) If you are 35 years or older (some may lower this to 30 years old)

If either or both of these scenarios above are true, then you are in a position where you cannot afford to put off investing for your future, even at the expense of slowing down your debt cancellation. In these scenarios, it is still imperative that you aggressively pursue eliminating your debt, but at the same time, you also need to be investing an appropriate amount into your retirement account. You will read in a later chapter all about the ideal investment strategy based upon your age, but if you are still paying off debt past the age of 35, then you will want to start investing right away. This should be at least half of the recommended amount for your age from Table 1 (on pages 91-92). Once your debt is paid off, you will want to increase your monthly investing to at least the fully recommended amount.

## GROUP 3

If you are in group 3, then you are reading this book at just the right time! Congratulations! As someone just starting out, you have the amazing advantage of starting with a clean slate. Not only that, but you also have the advantage of time on your side. The longer you have to accumulate wealth (through the power of compounding interest, discussed later), the easier it is to do so!

Okay, so you are presumably in your late-teens or twenties. Let's assume that you have no debt and you have recently started your first "real job." Just to be clear though, if you did somehow seem to rack up some credit card debt or student loan debt while in college (which the majority of college graduates have), then your number one goal is to get rid of this debt with your newly acquired income. Here is a very good rule-of-thumb to go by: as soon as you start your new career, you should do everything you can to eliminate all debt (other than your primary home mortgage if you have one) as soon as possible.

For example, if your starting salary is $40,000 a year, and you have $15,000 in car/student loan debt, then you should aggressively eliminate this debt in the next 12-18 months. Trust me on this one. You will be glad you did! There is just something that happens in your heart and mind when you successfully pay off all "consumer debt" at a very young age. Many financial "experts" may disagree and tell you to start investing right away by instead taking 24-36 months to pay off the debt. However, something takes place "beyond the mathematics" when you really dig in and pay off debt, not to mention that you no longer carry the burden of a monthly payment or the risks that accompany it.

With that said, let's get back to the "no debt" starting point scenario for all of you in Group 3. The biggest question people ask at this point is "how can I accumulate the things I need without going into debt or having monthly payments?" The answer is easy! Yet the implementation is hard!

Let's say you need a car since you are no longer living at home or on campus. Your new income allows you to easily go out and buy a $20,000 vehicle and incur 5 years' worth of $400 monthly payments. Yes, you could do this, but it would be very unwise. Instead, the wise thing to do would be to temporarily use a family car or even use public transportation (for those of you working in a big city) until you can save up $2,000-$3,000 to pay cash for a reliable, used car. By doing this, you then allow yourself to start "pocketing" that $400 a month payment that your friends all have, and when the time is right (after a few years of saving), upgrade your car to a $5000-$10,000 car and again pay cash for it!

Consider this example, if you will. Your friend goes out and buys a brand new Toyota, Ford or Nissan for $20,000, and comes home with a wonderful $400 monthly payment. Along with "owning" this fabulous car payment, they also get to go to sleep each night with the risk of repossession if they fail to make their payment for whatever reason. On top of that, they get reminded each month that their hard-earned money is actually worth $400 less because they have to send that amount to the car company. And if that wasn't enough, within 18 months their car is actually worth less than $15,000, so if they wanted to sell it, they would likely lose money on the sale. Once they do sell it (or trade it in), they have no money saved for another car, so they have to go out and get another loan with another $400 car payment, and the never-ending cycle continues. They will always live each month with $400 less than they actually make.

On the other hand, you decide to take a different approach. You use public transportation or a family car for the first 12 months. In that time, you save $400 a month in a "car fund." At the end of the year, you have $4,800. You then take that money and get a great deal on an 8-year old Toyota with only 100,000 miles on it.

(This car is extremely durable and dependable, and will last you at least another 100,000 miles if you want it to.) You will have no car debt and no worries over not being able to make a loan payment. In the meantime, you continue to save $400 a month in your "car fund," with the goal of upgrading as soon as possible. Two years later you have $9,600 in your "car fund" (24 months of saving $400), and you are able to sell your (now 10-years old) car for $3,400. With the $13,000 in cash that you have ($9,600 + $3,400), you then use that money to buy a 3-year old Toyota. You are now driving the SAME car as your friend (granted three years later than when he started driving it), but you own your car outright, while your friend is still paying $400 a month for the next 2 years. By the time he finally pays his car off two years later, and you of course continue to save your $400 a month for those two years, you will both be driving the exact same car, yet you will have $9,600 in your pocket, and he will have $0. Wow!

If we go one step further, you could actually invest that $9,600 and be years ahead of your friend in terms of long-term wealth accumulation, all while driving the exact...same...car! And to think, this whole scenario played out because your friend just "had to have" that new car right away, instead of being insightful enough to delay this gratification for a few short years in order to stay ahead of the game and NEVER have to live with a car payment. By the way, that $9,600 invested with 35 years to grow, just became over $400,000! Looks like his brand new Toyota that he just couldn't wait for became your brand new, fully-loaded Bentley or Ferrari!

So you may be thinking, "now that I know how to get a car without acquiring debt, what about all of the other things in life that people tell me I just 'have to have'?" Great question! And the answer is equally as great: the exact same way! The car analogy is very straightforward, and uses big numbers, but every other purchase (with the only possible exception being your home) works the exact same way. There is essentially no single consumer item that you need so desperately that it cannot wait 6-12 months in order for you to purchase it in cash. Believe me when I say I know that the temptation is great, and that it is very easy to say "as long as I can easily afford the monthly payment, then I can afford to buy this." But I cannot stress enough the amazing power that accompanies an individual who can see the long-term value of saving up the cash before going out and buying an item.

This person realizes how valuable it is to wake up every morning without wondering if they are going to make enough money this month to cover their minimum credit card payment.

This person sees the incredible potential that lies within each and every dollar that is invested as part of their long-term wealth accumulation plan.

This person also creates a culture within their own heart and mind that takes pleasure in purchasing assets. These assets will grow their potential for future success, as opposed to liabilities, which will merely fulfill a present desire. When all is said and done, this type of person will simply not be stopped on their journey towards financial freedom!

# CHAPTER 4 – STUDENT LOANS

Let me briefly talk about student loan debt, particularly to my younger readers. If you are reading this and you already have tens of thousands of dollars in student loan debt (or more!), please do not be discouraged or upset at what I am going to say. Your situation is what it is and it cannot be undone. Instead, just go after that debt with intensity and get it paid off as soon as possible!

For those of you who have no student loan debt or are in the midst of college as you read this, let me sincerely encourage you to stay as far away from this debt as possible. For the vast majority of you, paying the tuition fees in cash each semester is actually attainable if you are willing to work your tail off and be of the mindset that student loans are simply not an option. This may mean having to earn $1,000 a month and transferring to (or enrolling in) a state school where the cost is currently less than $12,000 per year in most cases. If you think you "just have to" attend a private school with prestige (and a $40,000 per year tuition bill!), and you don't have the cash on hand to pay for it, then it is time to change your perception. The vast majority of degrees will give you the same education and same opportunities whether you attend a state school or a private school. Having $100,000 in private school student loan debt versus having no debt from a public university will make a significant difference in your ability to save and invest throughout your 20s and 30s. In other words, being able to invest $700 a month, versus having a $700 monthly student loan payment, turns into over $1 million approximately 25 years down the road (which is how long most people continue to pay their student loan payment)!

For those of you who are pursuing advanced degrees (Master's, PhD, DDS, MD, etc.), then your situation becomes quite a bit more challenging. Across the board, you will find people who tell you that student loans are the only way to pay for these. Not true!

In the medical field, there are many universities that offer MD/PhD or DDS/PhD programs that will pay for your entire tuition in exchange for the research work that you provide them in the PhD portion of your program.

If an MBA is what you are after, there are countless companies that will pay the entire bill on your behalf either before or while you are employed by the company. This often requires a designated number of years that you will work for them, which is easily worth the benefits of a free Master's degree!

For other professions such as Lawyer/Attorney (JD), Physical Therapist (DPT), Physician's Assistant (PA-C), Veterinarian (DVM), Chiropractor (DC), Psychologist (PsyD), Pharmacist (PharmD) and so on, if you absolutely want to obtain these degrees without a burden of debt (in most cases between $100,000-$200,000), then you must be willing to make major sacrifices. The most common sacrifice is simply delaying the start of the program for a full year or two until you can earn at least half of the total cost of the degree. By doing this, you can then continue to work while in school (most likely fewer hours than before you began the program) in order to have the cash to pay for the remaining balance of the cost. I fully appreciate the fact that this is far easier said than done, and in many cases it is even extremely difficult. But I also appreciate the financial opportunities that are afforded to young people with no student loan debt, and you may never quite understand that until you are living it!

# CHAPTER 5 – CREDIT CARDS

The topic of credit cards is a very delicate subject. There are obviously many points of view out there, all of which you have probably heard. The reality of the situation is that over 46% of American households currently have credit card debt, and the average amount for those households is $15,480.[1] Furthermore, approximately 35% of Americans have consumer debt (mostly in the form of credit cards) that is in default, according to a study by the Urban Institute.

This information would tend to suggest that Americans should start adopting the stance taken by Dave Ramsey, which says that you should cut up your credit cards and never use them again. This point of view is enticing for several reasons:

1) If you don't use credit cards, then you will never amass credit card debt!

2) Several studies have shown that by using credit cards (or "plastic" in general), you will end up spending anywhere from 5%-20% more over the course of the year.

3) If you spend only the money that you have on hand, you are more likely to think about each and every purchase before it is made.

While these are very compelling arguments, especially when it comes to the success rate of your long-term financial plans, you will still find that many people will argue in favor of having credit cards. Their arguments include:

1) Having a credit card and paying off the balance every month is an easy way to increase your credit score and/or keep it high.

2) Rewards such as cash back or airline miles are nice bonuses for those who are responsible enough to never keep a balance on their card.

3) If emergency situations ever arise that require a substantial amount of money, only a credit card will allow you to immediately take care of the situation.

These are compelling arguments when debating the topic of credit cards. While I am not aiming to force an opinion on you, I will say that I am almost completely in favor of *avoiding* credit cards at all costs. The reason I say this is because I have seen and heard countless stories of people who told themselves that they would never get into credit card debt because they would pay the balance off every month. However, they ultimately found themselves in tens of thousands of dollars of debt several years later. If these people would have avoided credit cards altogether by using cash or debit cards, their financial lives would look considerably different. Can you just imagine what the average American could accomplish in terms of saving and investing if they did not have to make minimum payments on $15,480 of credit card debt every month?

Here is something to consider: if you currently have a credit card and have NEVER paid interest on an unpaid balance or a single late-fee, then you are probably in the small minority of people who can responsibly handle a credit card. However, I would still like to bring to your attention the fact that you are likely spending 5%-20% more over the course of the year than if you would have used cash instead.

One more point I would like to discuss is your "credit score." A large percentage of people today carry and use a credit card in order to increase or maintain a high credit score. Their belief is that you cannot financially succeed in life without a high credit score. This is absolutely untrue. While having a low or poor credit score can be very limiting or even destructive financially speaking, having a credit score of 0 is quite different. If you have no debt of any kind, and do not use credit cards, then over the course of a year or two, your credit score will drop all the way down to 0. While this may prevent you from renting *some* apartments, or from getting the absolute best price on certain insurances, it will create more advantages in the long-run than disadvantages.

Having a credit score of 0 means that you have no debt, do not borrow money of any kind, and are extremely responsible with your finances. The number one concern people voice over having a credit score of 0 is not being able to get a home mortgage. I have two responses for this concern:

1) If you are truly going to live your life "debt-free," then you will never consider taking out a home mortgage (i.e. debt), but instead pay for your home in cash.

2) If you are living completely debt-free prior to purchasing a home, then you are still able to obtain a mortgage with a credit score of 0. This process is called "manual underwriting" and there are a few mortgage companies that will do this for you, if you truly have a score of 0.

To keep this chapter brief, you now have read the arguments for and against the use of credit cards. I still circle back to the fact that without a credit card in your wallet, then you have absolutely no chance of falling into credit card debt! Secondly, if you are interested in spending 5%-20% less, then going without a credit card is definitely the right option for you!

I fully understand that this is a very difficult situation for most people, since we live in a day and age where nearly 100% of our purchases are made with the swipe of a card. However, if there is even the slightest chance that you will be unable to maintain a $0 balance each and every month, then please stay away from credit cards at all costs!

1 – From nerdwallet.com, based on an analysis of Federal Reserve statistics and other government data.

# CHAPTER 6 - BUDGETING

"Being able to live well and still invest, no matter how much money you make, requires a high level of financial intelligence. Having a surplus is something you have to actively budget for."
– Robert T. Kiyosaki from "Increase Your Financial IQ"

Now that we have established how to live our lives free of debt, and with more income each month than expenses, there are a few diffcrent ways to ensure financial success with any given income, depending on your personality (discussed further in Chapter 8). The first way is the most commonly recommended approach, and that is to establish and abide by a detailed, written budget. Personal finance experts are almost all proponents of this. The reason being is that budgeting gives you a very specific understanding of where your money is going every month and allows you to develop a plan of action for how you want to spend your money. Whether you make $1,000 a month or $50,000 a month, having a game plan written out is the only way that you will truly be in control of where your money is going!

In his book "The Millionaire Next Door," author Stanley J. Thomas uses a very powerful sports analogy. He refers to your income as your *offense*, and a budget/plan as your *defense*. This is all in reference to the life-long "game" of building wealth. Some individuals have a high income and thus a great *offense*, yet they are so lacking on *defense* (they have no budget and no monthly plan for their money) that they come up dramatically short on fulfilling their potential in terms of wealth accumulation. But with a good-to-great *defense* in place, these people will no doubt become multi-millionaires.

At the same time, the vast majority of Americans have what many would consider an average income, and thus it may seem as though their *offense* is lacking. However, some of those very same people have developed a great *defense* (detailed budget that includes a strong saving and investing plan), and thus are able to far exceed their expected wealth accumulation levels. You see, a person with a great *offense* (income) that has little or no *defense* (budget/game plan) may or may not find success in their quest for long-term wealth accumulation. They will, however, fall substantially short in reaching their full potential. However, a person with an average *offense*, coupled with a stellar *defense*, will reach levels of wealth accumulation that are only dreamed about by the majority of their peers. This is because with enough time and dedication, even a seemingly small amount of money, when invested correctly and consistently, can produce vast amounts of wealth, and will result in complete financial independence!

Getting back to the budget itself, there are many books out there on creating a budget, and that is not the focus of this book, but here is an example of how a classic budget works.

First, you write down the exact amount of income (after taxes) that you will be receiving for the month. Next, you list each and every fixed expense that you know needs to be paid each month. This includes, but is not limited to: rent/mortgage, phone bill, cable bill, internet bill, insurance, utilities (can be a fixed amount if you use the average monthly payment plan commonly offered), car/credit card/student loan payment (if you still have debt), etc. You then assign a "budgeted" amount to the variable necessities in your life: food, gas, non-fixed utilities, etc. (use past months' expenses to get an accurate estimation as to what these amounts will be).

After you tally up all of your monthly expenses, both fixed and variable, you simply subtract that number from your total monthly income. With the money that remains (and if this total is $0, then you need to re-read Chapter 2), you then allot specific amounts to things such as clothes, eating out, entertainment, miscellaneous, etc. In this phase, it is absolutely crucial to also budget a specific amount for giving (i.e. charitable donations), saving and investing. If you do not budget for these last three items, they simply will not get done.

Giving, which in my opinion is the most important, is so that you develop your character in such a way that you take pleasure in giving back to your community (church, foundation, organization, etc.). You should also know that your donations can often be "tax deductible," as long as you are giving to a 501(c)(3) non-profit company or organization. Saving is for increasing your emergency fund, or for building up cash for a specific purchase. Investing, which we will cover in greater detail in later chapters, is primarily for retirement accounts that will not be touched until age 59 ½ or later. If you do not "budget" a certain amount to give, save and invest, you will find yourself using the following phrase: "But I just don't have/make enough money to be giving, saving or investing right now." I must say, without being too harsh, one of my goals in writing this book is that the people who read and implement the knowledge found on these pages will never have to say that phrase again for as long as they live!

In summary, after all of these categories are addressed in your budget, you will have ideally spent or allocated every dollar coming in each month. This ensures that you not only know where your money is going every month, but that you are the one in charge of telling it exactly where to go!

# CHAPTER 7 - HOUSING

As we move forward, let me briefly, yet emphatically, touch on the single largest item in everyone's budget: housing. Whether you are renting or own your home, this expense clearly represents the bulk of your monthly budget. Because of this fact, it is imperative that you keep this number under control and within your means.

In the following paragraphs I will continuously refer to your housing expenses as your "mortgage," but please realize that if you are renting, then you would simply replace the word "mortgage" with "rent."

First off, for the record, the absolute best way to purchase a home is to pay for the home entirely in cash. I realize that about 90% of the people who read that last sentence disregarded it as impossible. Well, if that is your opinion, then you are probably correct, it is impossible...for you. However, if you believe in yourself and your ability to get out of and stay out of debt forever, then you are very likely to own a home one day without debt, and then ultimately purchase a future home entirely with cash.

That being said, obtaining a mortgage in order to purchase your first home is a fact of life for the vast majority of Americans, including myself. When determining the appropriate price for the house you are going to buy, it is really very simple. Your monthly mortgage payment should not be more than 25% of your gross monthly salary (many would argue that this number should be 25% of your *take-home* or *net* monthly salary). Second, the type of loan that you get should be a 15-year, fixed-rate mortgage. And finally, you should have a down payment equal to 20% or more of the purchase price. If you follow these three rules, then your budgeted amount for housing will never be out of line, and thus will not bring you unwanted stress.

When budgeting 25% (or less) of your monthly income for a mortgage, the total payment that you are considering should include your principal, interest, taxes and insurance. For a typical mortgage, the payment that you make goes partially to pay down the principal (actual amount of the loan) and partially to pay the interest. If your taxes and insurance are not already included in your mortgage payment (escrowed), then you will need to account for these as well. (For those of you who are renting, simply add together your rent payment and any renter's insurance that you may be paying).

The mistake many Americans make (just look at the recession of 2009), is that their monthly housing expense is far more than they can handle. Loan officers will offer you many different kinds of loans, all of which will carry with them lower monthly payments than the 15-year, fixed-rate mortgage, but they also bring with them greater risk and longer amounts of time in debt!

Let's briefly define what a 15-year, fixed-rate mortgage is. A mortgage with a fixed rate means that the interest rate on the loan will not change, and the monthly payment you make today will always stay the same for the life of the loan. There are other types of loans called "adjustable rate mortgages" (ARM), which have the monthly payment fixed for a specific number of years. After this period ends, the loan rate is adjusted and the monthly payment increases by an unknown amount. These types of loans are what get people in serious trouble. They think they can afford the payment for the first few years, but when the interest rate "adjusts" and the payment increases by $300 a month (for example), they no longer can afford it and are ultimately faced with a short-sale or foreclosure. And in the midst of it all, they struggle to cover their other monthly expenses and ultimately see the amount of stress in their lives drastically rise.

The "15-year" part means that if you make the required payment each and every month, then the loan will be paid in full in exactly 15 years. Fixed-rate loans are usually 15-years or 30-years in duration. For example, let's say your neighbor has a 30-year loan on his $200,000 house. At the same time, you have a 15-year loan on your $200,000 house. Although his monthly payment will be $400 less than yours, he will be making his payments for 30 years, while your house will be completely paid off in only 15 years. Because your neighbor has to make his payment for an additional 15 years compared to you (and because 30-year loans always have a higher interest rate), his loan is actually costing him over $100,000 more than yours over the life of the loan!

**NOTE:** If you currently have a 30-year fixed-rate mortgage on your home, then by simply paying one additional payment each year (towards the principal) you can pay off your 30-year loan in approximately 25 years. If you make two additional payments each year, then you can pay off your 30-year loan in less than 21 years!

With all that said, please remember these "rules" and make it a point to follow them no matter what other options are presented to you. Make no mistake about it, a mortgage company will figure out the maximum that *they* think you can afford based on your salary and other debts. This is the first step to really getting yourself maxed out in terms of your monthly budget. Even if the bank says you can "afford" a mortgage payment that is 50% of your monthly salary, and with only a 5% down payment, know that the resulting size of this payment will substantially reduce your ability to save and invest on a monthly basis. As we have discussed previously, the lower your monthly expenses, the greater your monthly surplus, which allows you the most opportunity to increase your long-term wealth accumulation.

I should mention that if you are unable to pay for your home in cash, there is one financial benefit to having a home mortgage. All of the interest that you pay throughout the year is able to be deducted from your taxes. However, this is not a good reason for you to keep a home mortgage if you have the ability to pay it off early! Let's say for example that your overall mortgage payment is $1,000 per month, with about $500 of that being the interest payment (the other $500 being principal payment). At the end of the year you will have paid $6,000 in mortgage interest (12 x $500 = $6,000). You can then deduct this interest, and depending on your tax bracket, this would equate to roughly $2,000 in tax savings (33% of $6,000 = $2,000). So basically, in order to save $2,000 in taxes at the end of the year, you have agreed to pay $6,000 in interest on your home mortgage. This doesn't sound like that great of a deal to me. If you had no mortgage payment at all, you could instead give an extra $6,000 to your favorite charity or even invest an extra $6,000 in a tax-deductible investment account, both of which will give you the same tax deduction that a mortgage payment would.

One final word of caution. If you are in the home-buying phase of your life, please beware that many people use unwise justifications to convince themselves that they can "afford" the monthly payment. The two most common are 1) co-signors and 2) renters/roommates. If the bank you are working with requires a parent or relative (i.e. anyone other than your spouse) to co-sign the loan with you, then you CANNOT afford that loan! The bank obviously knows this, which is why they need someone else to be responsible for the payment if you fail to pay it.

In terms of live-in renters or roommates, if the only way you can "afford" your monthly payment is by having someone rent a room or an area of your home, then again, you CANNOT afford that home. I have no problem with you making "extra" income by having a renter, but if you are relying on their payment in order to help you pay your mortgage, then you are asking for trouble.

# CHAPTER 8 – PAY YOURSELF FIRST

Another method of motivating your money on a monthly basis would be a so-called "reverse-budget." This has been around at least since the days of George Clason's 1926 book "The Richest Man in Babylon." It is summed up in the three-word expression: Pay Yourself First. The premise behind this concept is very simple: at the beginning of every month (or once you deposit each individual paycheck) you are to take a certain percentage for "yourself." In other words, before any of your money is spent, you will have donated (given), saved and invested your desired amount, thus making it impossible to "not have enough money" for these to happen. One of the models derived from this method is the "10-10-10-70 System." What this breaks down to is that 10% of your income is given away (tithe/charity), 10% goes to your emergency savings account, 10% goes to investing for retirement and the remaining 70% is what you live on.

To most people reading this book, living off of only 70% of one's income sounds like an unattainably low figure. I fully understand this point of view, but let's talk about it first before we dismiss it as impossible. Here is a decent analogy that I like to use: the typical American sleeps for 8 hours in a given 24-hour period, and thus has 16 hours to "budget" however he or she may choose. For most, 9 hours are devoted to our job (depending on your commute time), therefore we really only have 7 hours each day to allocate for ourselves. If you are like most Americans, even though on paper we may have 7 hours to do whatever we please, we still inevitably complain each night, "Where did the day go?" Or better yet, "If only I had an extra two hours each day, because there just isn't enough time to get everything done!"

With those numbers in mind, let's use the example of the person who for the past 15 years has allotted 30 minutes each day to prayer and meditation, along with 60 minutes each day to exercise. This person still works 40 hours a week and sleeps a full 8 hours each night. How can it be possible, that in a world where everyone is complaining about not having enough time in their day, that this person can spend 90 minutes of each day on "themselves"? The answer: because they have made the decision that these things must be done, and then they "budget" the rest of their day accordingly. Because they put such a high priority on this time, instead of mindlessly flipping through television channels or perusing social media websites, they now have no problem getting the most out of their time each day.

Now I know this may not be a perfect analogy, but you get the point! Whatever finite resource we are talking about, whether money, time, mental capacity, etc., once you place a priority on how you use it and you make that allotment a habit or custom, then you eventually learn to make do with what you have left.

This is exactly how the "pay yourself first" theory works. What it really takes is self-discipline and proper prioritization to make it work. Once you determine in your head and in your heart that you are going to apply this principle, it quickly becomes your new way of life, and the difficulty seems to fade away. Furthermore, when you put aside this money before anything else happens, you ensure that it will actually happen! When you save these expenditures for the "end" of your budget, you will quickly find that you do not have the full 30% to allocate to these areas, and before you know it, you will ultimately have no money at the end of each month to give, save or invest.

Consider this: if you were a brand new college graduate, used to making $100 per week, and I told you I would hire you full-time for $700 a week, could you live off of that? Of course you could! What if I then told you, I'm actually going to be paying you $1,000 a week, but I will only give you the job if you take the first 30% to give, save and invest. Could you make that work? Again, of course! This is because you started from square one not depending on that additional 30%!

"But Russell, how can you expect me to live on 70% of my current income, when for the past 10+ years I have barely been surviving on 100%?"

I don't *expect* you to live on 70%, I am simply telling you that if you want a fail-proof way to get WAY ahead in your path toward wealth accumulation, that this is a tried and true formula to accomplish just that.

To be less blunt about it, going from living on 100% to 70% of your income overnight is pretty much impossible for the vast majority of Americans. What I would encourage you to do is to start with 1% giving, 1% saving, 1% investing and living on 97%. This may take a drastic reduction in debt just to get to this level. It may take a paradigm shift in your lifestyle. Regardless of "how" you get there, you must set the goal of actually getting there! Once you have gotten that under your belt, then shoot for 5% giving, 5% saving, 5% investing and living on 85%. This process of shifting from 100% down to 70% may take you three months or three years! No matter how long it takes you, as long as you are committed to the goal, it will without a doubt change your financial future forever!

"Okay, so I see your point Russell, but why would I want to give up so much of my money every month, and further, how can I do this if I have been living so long without doing it?"

Great questions!

By reading this book thus far, I hope you have determined that the absolute best way to build up wealth is to maximize the amount of money that you invest into your "Asset Bucket" every month.

Whether this is stock market investing, business investing or real-estate investing, the only way any of this is possible (without going into debt of course) is to have as much money left over at the end of every month. By living on as little as 70% of what you earn, you are able to allocate a higher percentage to areas that will one day bring in "passive income," which is money that you make regardless of the amount of time you spend "working." In order for you to fully appreciate the value of this concept, you must be able to look beyond the present and see the possibilities that are afforded to the person that has their money working for them, instead of them working for their money. This phenomenon is absolutely possible if you are committed in your earlier years to building your assets as wisely as possible.

Without question, the biggest hurdle that most Americans face in dealing with this issue is the fact that you must be willing and able to delay the "normal pleasures" that this world has to offer, in exchange for future wealth and comfort. This is far easier said than done. When people all around you are buying bigger homes, financing nicer cars, joining country clubs, eating out every weekend and going on lavish vacations, you must not only be content with your financial game plan, but also be convinced that a bountiful surplus of resources in your 60s and beyond is far more precious than temporary pleasures in the present.

I personally like the farming example when it comes to "paying yourself first." This analogy is also pervasive throughout the Bible when it teaches about sowing your time, talent and finances in expectation of a harvest.

In terms of farming, let's use corn as our example. Every farmer knows that corn seed that is just sitting in the bag will never produce a harvest. The key to the harvest is to go out months beforehand and actually plant or sow the seed. Once harvest time arrives, all of the corn is gathered and then divided up based on the quality of the corn. This is where the analogy gets fascinating in my opinion! The farmer takes the very best portion of his corn, and sets it aside to use as seed for next year's crop. He then takes the next best portion and sets that aside to sell in order to provide financially for his family. Finally, he takes the remaining portion to feed his family.

The obvious financial lesson to be learned here is the importance of prioritizing your income or "harvest"! Whether you view the farmer planting the first portion of his harvest as "giving" or "investing," the principle still remains. When the harvest comes in, his first priority is to take a significant portion for giving, saving and investing. It is only AFTER this has been done that he allows himself and his family to consume the rest. I realize that this is not a perfect analogy, especially for any professional farmers that may be reading this book, but I trust that you understand the principle!

In our culture today, our first priority is to consume as much of our income as we can until all of our desires are met. We have such a "spend first" mentality that it is without a doubt the number one reason for the lack of personal wealth accumulation in our society. Without a shift in this mentality, the only way a person will ever become wealthy is to have an extremely high salary. This phenomenon of financial imbalance has played itself out for generations, and has convinced the majority of Americans that earning an extremely high salary is in fact the only way to become wealthy in your lifetime.

If you can take away just one thing from this book, it would be this: it is absolutely vital that you make it an unwavering, non-debatable way of life to give, save and invest as the first priority in your personal budget. If you can achieve this paradigm shift, and I know you can, then you will ensure yourself a life of financial success.

# CHAPTER 9 – GIVING

Okay, so now you believe that giving, saving and investing "can" be done and "why" they should be done, let's talk more about each of them specifically.

The first 10% of the "10-10-10-70 System" is giving. To many people, giving away 10% seems ridiculously high and unnecessary, especially for someone who wants to "accumulate" wealth. However, I have found that it is an essential part of your financial game plan. The Biblical principal that says "it is better to give than to receive" is not just a centuries-old proverb, it really does do something to you mentally, emotionally and spiritually. By freely giving to a charitable cause, church or goodwill organization, you learn quickly the counterintuitive truth that keeping a firm grasp on all of your money is not the best way to maximize its growth. When you start to impact the lives of those around you, you begin to see the power of generosity. The Bible refers to this 10% as the tithe, and promises "more blessings than you can contain" to those who give with a cheerful heart (2 Corinthians 9:7-8 & Malachi 3:10). Even if you do not read or believe the Bible, the principle still holds true, like it or not! Nearly every highly successful individual that teaches on wealth accumulation will, without fail, mention the fact that donating a portion of your income is absolutely essential to financial success. If anything else, giving helps to eliminate the life-destroying emotion of greed! Because ultimately greed leads to devastation and ruin.

Even though you experience an emotional high when you see your money accumulating, I assure you that it will not compare to the emotional high you will receive when you take the money you have been blessed with and enhance the life of someone else. You would be very surprised to know just how much $1,000 or even $100 can change a person's current situation for the better. Furthermore, the charities, religious groups and non-profit organizations, of which provide life-changing services to those in your community, country and around the world, each rely almost exclusively on the financial contributions of people just like you and me. If you have dismissed the notion that you, by yourself, can make a difference in the needs of those around you (and thus have given up on even trying), then let me convince you otherwise. Whether it is $10, $100 or $1,000, your financial contribution to a worthy cause does in fact make a major difference when combined with the efforts of others doing the same thing.

As we briefly discussed earlier, one of the purely mathematical advantages to giving is that it can often be 100% tax deductible. What this means is that if you are contributing to 501(c)(3) organization (church, charity, etc.), then this money can be donated without the government taxing it! This a great way to support a worthy cause without having taxes limit your hard-earned money!

Finally, without the "giving component" in your financial game plan, you will be missing a major catalyst to your long-term success. Mathematics alone cannot account for the role that giving plays, and a life of financial success without a certain element of giving will leave you with a gaping void that mere money cannot fulfill!

# CHAPTER 10 – SAVING

Now, the second 10% of the "10-10-10-70 System" needs to be allocated to a personal savings account. It is amazing to see the statistics on the average household's savings accounts. I truly believe that a staggering amount of stress would be eliminated from our lives if we simply had an adequate savings account (i.e. emergency fund) to get us through those unexpected financial road blocks.

Here is the rule-of-thumb where this is concerned: if you want to live far more securely than the average American, then you should have at least 6 months of living expenses saved in a fully-insured (FDIC) savings account. For most people, we can conservatively estimate that half of your annual income is spent on required living expenses for the year, while the other half goes to taxes and other miscellaneous spending. In order to save enough to cover 6 months of these expenses, your savings account should ultimately be equal to at least 25% of your gross annual income.

If you are saving a full 10% of your income each month into this account, then at the end of the first year, you will have 10% of your annual salary saved. If you continue this for 2.5 years (30 months), then you will have saved 25% of your annual salary into your emergency fund, or 6 full months of living expenses. Once you reach this point you will be done with the 10% saving portion of your "pay yourself first" budget! (FYI, if you do this for 5 years, then you will have saved 50% of your yearly income, which would in essence be a full year of living expenses!).

For example, if you make $50,000 a year, the breakdown should look like this (if you are following the plan laid out in this book):

$10,000 – taxes (20% - usually taken out of your paycheck)

$25,000 – everyday expenses for the year (50%)

$5,000 – giving (10%)

$5,000 – saving (10%)

$5,000 – investing (10%)

**NOTE:** Saving 10% of your salary (or $5,000) each year for 2.5 years will give you an emergency fund of $12,500, which is equal to 6 months of expenses.

The money in your emergency fund should be in a high-yield savings account or a money market account (as of this writing, this would mean about a 1.0% annual interest rate). This should absolutely not, in any way, be linked to your everyday checking and savings accounts (which are only used for short-term purchases and expenses)!

Anywhere from 6 to 12 months of expenses is ideal (or 25%-50% of you annual income), depending on your level of comfort, but it is my opinion that anything less than 6 months is too low. One way to look at it is from this perspective: with an over-funded emergency fund, you would have the extra money to use if an extraordinary situation or opportunity arises, such as an emergency concerning a loved one, funding a job transition or starting a new business. None of these would be possible if you only had 3 months' worth of expenses in your savings account.

No matter what your annual salary is, once you have achieved this extraordinary feat of saving 6-12 months' worth of expenses (or

25% - 50% of your annual income), the question then becomes "what should you do next?" The answer: take the 10% that you were saving and add it to your giving and investing accounts!

This leads us to the last 10% of the "10-10-10-70 System," which is investing! This is either a scary word to you or an exciting word! Let me assure you, once you fully understand what the whole "investing world" is all about, it will become far more exciting than scary!

# PART II - Investing

## CHAPTER 11 – BASICS OF INVESTING

Finally, the last 10% of the "10-10-10-70 System" is for investing. To many, the thought of investing conjures up negative thoughts or emotions. Why is there so much negativity surrounding the concept of investing? Well, there are many reasons. Some may have had a loved one, or even themselves, lose a great deal of money on what was sold to them as a "can't miss investment." Some may believe that investing in the stock market is nothing more than mere gambling. Others may just feel overwhelmed by putting their money into something that they do not understand or that they think is only for "rich people."

First off, the number one rule of investing is that you should never invest your money into something that you do not *adequately* understand. Regardless of where your information comes from, even if you read it in a book (like this one!), you simply should not put your money into something that you know little or nothing about.

For the purpose of this book, there are really only five areas where 99% of Americans should even consider investing their money: private businesses, real estate, stocks, bonds and mutual funds. Before we discuss each of these, let's first clear the air by defining what "investing" actually means.

As you will recall from chapter 8, investing should be something that is done (or budgeted for) every single month, and the goal should be no less than 10% of your gross income. If you use the "pay yourself first" analogy, this investment money is, in essence, set aside right away when money comes in. This way, there is no question as to whether or not you have enough to invest at the end of the month. If we are using the "bucket analogy" (although this money is technically taken from the surplus that remains after mandatory expenses are paid), it should *almost* be prioritized above your "Expenses Bucket." As we talked about previously, the vast majority of people who have money remaining after paying monthly expenses end up spending this money on liabilities instead of assets. However, those people who are serious about long-term wealth accumulation are those that place a much higher priority on investing in order to increase their assets as opposed to wasting money on liabilities. With that being said, investing can simply be defined as "increasing one's assets" (i.e. anything that increases in value over time), and we will discuss the various ways to do this in the following chapters.

# CHAPTER 12 – PRIVATE BUSINESS

Investing in a private business (either your own business or a start-up business that is looking to you as an outside investor or financial partner) can be a very complicated topic to discuss. For the purposes of this book, we are going to keep it very simple. First off, investing in your own business can be extremely profitable, can end up as a total loss, or can fall somewhere in between. When you invest in your own business, whether that is purchasing a franchise, inventory accumulation, patent applications, equipment, marketing, etc., the return on your investment depends on how successfully you run that business.

Obviously there is an inherent motivation to see your own company succeed at any cost, and thus you may have an unrealistic view on the actual level of success attainable. If you have a serious passion for starting and investing in your own business, I am certainly not here to dissuade you! I am very much pro-entrepreneurship, and think it can be a very wise investment. However, I highly recommend that you enlist the services of a competent and experienced accountant and small business attorney before beginning this venture.

The second possibility to discuss would be investing in a business as an outsider. The most common form of this is when a family member or close friend is involved, of which great caution is required. Again, this can be a very wise investment if the business is operated efficiently and the overall model of the business is sound and unique. These are often referred to as "start-up companies," and they are looking to investors in order to raise money, or capital, to help get their business off the ground. In return for your money, you are often given a percentage of ownership in the company (often expressed as "shares"). You will then receive a portion of the annual profit based on your percentage of ownership. If the company does well, your yearly percentage could yield you a very high return on your investment (ROI). You would also have the opportunity to sell your percentage of the company for a much higher price than you paid, thus giving you a large profit on your original investment. Again, taking part in any investment opportunity of this nature involves a great deal of up-front knowledge, and should involve the counsel of experienced accountants and/or attorneys.

Finally, when investing in a business, please do not underappreciate the fact that there is a very high chance (maybe even higher than 50% depending on which statistics you believe) that this business may not succeed and thus you could lose 100% of your investment. If you are willing and able to take this inherent risk, then this type of investment may very well turn into an incredible source of long-term wealth.

# CHAPTER 13 – REAL ESTATE

As with investing in private business, real estate investing can also produce a very high rate of return, yet it too has its own high levels of risk. Again, this is not the focus of this book, so a very brief overview and generalization will be discussed here. If real estate investing is something that you feel strongly drawn to, then you should get your hands on as many additional resources as you can after reading this book.

For our purposes, real estate can be broken down into three simple categories: residential, commercial and land. For the vast majority of people reading this book, these are the only three types of real estate that you will ever need to consider investing in. Residential real estate includes properties in which individuals or families rent from you on a monthly or yearly basis. Commercial real estate would be various types of buildings that other businesses lease from you. Land would be pieces of property that do not contain structures, but can be leased from you for farming purposes or mineral rights (such as drilling for oil or other natural resources). Of course, each of these can ultimately be sold for a profit as well.

Of these three categories, residential is by far the most common form of real estate investing done by the general public, and the one that we will focus on for the duration of this chapter.

There are two primary ways that residential real estate can make a profit for the investor: rental income and/or profit from selling. A typical "rental property" is very simple in theory. An investor first determines the type of property that they are interested in purchasing. This can be an apartment, condo, townhome, duplex or single-family home (to name a few). In evaluating the type of property, one must take into account several key variables. The most important of which are location, price, "rent-ability" and potential for long-term appreciation. Purchasing an investment property must be a well-researched endeavor, especially to find a property which has a high rating on each of these variables.

As for the location, you will certainly want this property to be in a very desirable area of town, as this will yield the highest monthly rent and have the greatest chance to garner a high selling price in the future.

At the same time, the price of the property that you are considering is extremely important in determining whether or not this will be a successful investment. It is often said that when investing in real estate the real profit of the investment takes place when you buy the property, not when you sell it. In other words, if you are able to purchase a property at a price that is substantially below that of market value, then you essentially have secured your profit right then and there. Whether you rent this property or sell it rather quickly, a lower buying price will cause your rental income to be a higher percentage of profit, or will allow for maximum profit when sold.

Since we are talking about the buying price, we need to discuss the various purchasing options that are available. To keep it simple, you can either purchase real estate with cash, or you can take out a loan that requires you to make payments. There are countless stories of people gaining great wealth and success by using both methods, but for the record, I am only going to be endorsing the purchasing of real estate as an all-cash deal (meaning no debt is involved).

When you buy a property with cash, you immediately take full ownership of the property and thus eliminate the vast majority of risk associated with the investment. You have no obligation to make payments to anyone, and any rental income that you receive is basically 100% profit on your investment. For example, let's say you purchase a rental property for $100,000 cash, and you are able to rent it out for $1,000 a month. Without factoring in any additional costs to maintain the property (of which there are many!), this would produce a profit of $12,000 a year (12 months x $1,000), which in turn represents a 12% annual return on your investment! Without getting too in depth, you must also consider the cost of property taxes, insurance, repairs, management fees (unless you do this yourself), and any other miscellaneous fees that may arise. Even if these amount to $2,000 per year, you are still making a profit of $10,000 per year, or a 10% annual return on your investment.

Now, the one disadvantage of this method is that you will have to save the total amount of the purchase price before you are able to pay cash for this investment. Whether this is a $50,000 property or a $500,000 property, this is still a very large amount of money to save. On top of that, you must be mentally willing to see all of that money "disappear" from your account and be placed into your property. This of course means that you no longer have immediate access to this money, and the only way you can get it all back is to sell your property (which is not always a very easy proposition).

On the other hand, and as many real estate investing books would recommend, you can go out to your bank and take out a secured loan (mortgage) on your property. This in turn will require a monthly payment to be paid back to the bank. There are several things to consider here. With monthly loan payments, you are forfeiting a large percentage of your rental profit each month. If your monthly loan payment is $800, and you receive $1,000 per month in rent, then your profit is only $200 per month. On top of this, your monthly loan payments are due each and every month, so if you have a month where your renter does not pay, or if your renter decides to break their lease and leave, you are still required to make that loan payment, which in that case would cause you to have a financial loss that month. This may or may not seem to be high risk to you, but I have seen many people ultimately lose their rental property to foreclosure simply because they could not keep their property rented for whatever reason.

Taking out a loan to purchase a rental property obviously has its disadvantages. However, on the flip side, this method only requires a fraction of your own cash up front in order to complete the transaction, which usually amounts to a down payment and closing costs. On a $100,000 property, your up-front cost may be as little as $5,000 total. Of course, if you actually have the full $100,000 available in cash and still want to take out a loan, this method would allow you to keep the remaining $95,000.

As you can see, there are many ways in which real estate investments can be made, and the amount of risk you are willing to take depends entirely on you and your financial situation. As I stated before, it is my intention to recommend real estate investing only when it can be done by paying for the property in cash. There is minimal risk of financial ruin (foreclosure, bankruptcy, etc.) when you are dealing with an investment property that is completely paid for!

Now back to the variables that make for a wise real estate investment. The location, as well as the surrounding amenities, safety of the neighborhood, school district, etc. all play into the "rent-ability" of the property. The more desirable your property is, the more likely it is to stay rented each and every year, and the more likely it is to demand top dollar in monthly rent. This also dictates just how much the value of the property will increase over the long-term, thus allowing for the greatest return on your investment if you were to sell it down the road. If all of these variables come into place, then you are much more likely to have a successful investment in your portfolio.

Finally, as mentioned earlier, the other way to make a profit from residential real estate is by quickly turning around and selling the property for more than it was purchased for. This is often referred to as "flipping." Countless individuals have become very wealthy through this process, but at the same time, a far greater number have become bankrupt or financially ruined through it as well. The variables we just discussed can all be applied to this investment strategy as well, yet with a slightly different point of view in that renters are not likely to be involved. As previously mentioned, you should purchase the property for a low price (a rule of thumb should be no more than 80% of the current market value), it should be in a great location, and there should be a strong market for this type of property in terms of people wanting to buy it.

When flipping a house, the only additional variable that must be discussed is that of "adding value." Beyond the purchase price, this is likely the single most important variable for increasing the profitability of the transaction. This means that you can maximize your profit by either renovating, remodeling or restoring the property to a condition that warrants a much higher sale price than what you originally purchased it for. The most common success stories from those in the house flipping business occur when a distressed (run-down, abandoned, deteriorated) property is purchased at a rock-bottom price (often less than 50% of the market value of surrounding properties), fixed-up and restored, and then re-sold for a premium price.

Buying with cash or taking out a loan also plays a factor in how much money you can spend on adding value to the property, and how long you can afford to wait until you sell it. If loan payments are required during each month of this flipping process, then this can substantially eat into your profits when you ultimately sell.

If this is process is done right, it can lead to a return on your investment of 100% or more in a matter of months. Of course, for every 1 investor that flips a property and makes a 100% profit, there are likely 5 or more investors that lose money doing the exact same thing. The key to making this a wise and successful investment is doing your due-diligence on the front end to make sure that all of the factors previously discussed have been taken into account. You must also make wise decisions on how much money is spent on the improvements that are made to increase the value of the home. On paper, this sounds very appealing and straightforward, but as any experienced real estate investor can tell you, there are many variables that will unexpectedly come into play. In light of this, extreme caution and diligence must be taken when it comes to flipping a house.

# CHAPTER 14 - STOCKS

We are now entering the area of investing where we will spend the duration of our time...the stock market!

The average person will react in one of three ways when they hear the term "stock market": 1) that's only for rich people and way beyond my understanding, 2) that's nothing more than "big-business gambling" and I want nothing to do with other people stealing my money, or 3) that's the best place to invest my money in order to achieve long-term wealth accumulation.

If you are reading this book, you more than likely have one of these opinions, or a combination of them. Regardless of how you feel about the stock market, the remainder of this book will enlighten and educate you to the point where you will be, at the very least, well-informed when it comes to stock market investing.

To make sure that we are all on the same page, I will first give you a brief overview of stocks and the stock market. A *stock* simply represents ownership of a company. You will commonly hear a person say, "I own stock in that company." A *share* is simply an amount of *stock* that a person is able to purchase, and has a value (or share price) that goes up and down based on how successful the company is. For example, if I wanted to purchase Google stock, I could buy 10 shares of stock, for $550 per share, which would cost me $5,500.

The stock market is the collection of all the companies (in America and around the world) that are available for the general public to invest in. These companies are also known as "publically traded companies." This means that they have *shares* of their company *stock* available for the public to buy and sell on the *stock market*. Generally speaking, as the company financially increases, then the price per share of the company also increases. At the same time, the exact opposite is true, which results in the share price decreasing as the company financially decreases.

Before moving on, I should mention that the stock market is also commonly referred to as the "equities market." If you ever hear the term "equities" or "equities market" mentioned, just know that this is referring to the stocks of publically traded companies, both in America and internationally (often called "international equities").

Stocks can be sold individually (i.e. buying a single share of stock in a particular company), or grouped together in a mutual fund (shares of stocks from multiple companies all lumped together under one "umbrella"). If you buy shares in one company, then all of your money goes up and down exactly in line with how that particular company performs. If you buy shares of a mutual fund (which contains multiple companies), then all of your money goes up or down in proportion to how the entire group of companies within that mutual fund performs. Mutual funds will be discussed further in chapter 16.

In general, there are two "markets" that you can invest in: the "stock market" and the "bond market." The "bond market" covers all of the different types of bonds that are available to purchase, and will be discussed in the next chapter.

# CHAPTER 15 – BONDS

Bonds can be very complicated to explain and analyze, which is why I highly encourage you to talk with a financial professional to discuss the many different types of bonds available and how to go about investing in them. With that being said, bonds are one of the lower risk investments available today. However, with that lower risk comes one of the lowest returns (historically) on your investment over the long run.

As previously discussed, owning a share of stock means you own a portion of the company, but owning a bond means the company is "bonded" to pay you a certain amount of interest regardless of how well the company performs. As a result, there is much less risk and also much less reward by owning a bond.

In order to keep things simplified, when you purchase a bond, you are essentially loaning money to an institution (government, corporation, etc.), and in return they pay you a certain annual percentage (interest) on your money. This interest rate has fluctuated over the decades, but historically it has ranged from 1% to 5%. For the purpose of educating the investor, bonds should be looked at as an investment option while keeping the following three points in mind:

1) They carry a lower risk, with a return of approximately 1% to 5%.

2) Their average rate of return will not dramatically increase your investment portfolio (like stocks could potentially do), yet at the same time they will not dramatically decrease your portfolio either.

3) The percentage of bonds in your investment portfolio should be proportional to the amount of time you have before retirement and how much risk you are or are not willing to take.

Now that you have the information above, I will briefly discuss the two theories that exist in terms of "whether or not" and "how much" to invest in bonds. The first theory, and much more widely accepted, is that you should in fact invest a specific proportion of your portfolio into bonds. The second theory says that bonds basically put a strangle-hold on the growth potential of your investment portfolio and should be avoided.

**BOND THEORY ONE**

If you follow theory one, then the question you will want to ask is "what percentage of my investment portfolio should I have in bonds?"

There is not a hard and fast rule for this, but from all of my research, this is what I believe is the best formula to follow:

"You Current Age – 25 = Percentage of Your Portfolio in Bonds"

My personal caveat would be to not implement this formula until you reach the age of 40, as it will substantially slow down your overall portfolio growth. In simple terms, if you are younger than 40 years old, then there is no need for you to be invested in bonds. Because you have so much time before you reach retirement, you can easily handle the risks associated with the ups and down of the stock market.

For the typical 40 year old, this would mean that you should have approximately 15% of your portfolio in bonds (40 years old – 25 = 15%). This will protect a small percentage of your investments from any major stock market downturn, but again you have 20-25 more years to absorb the fluctuation in the market, and thus should have the vast majority of your money in "equities" (stocks).

For the typical 50 year old, this would mean that you should have approximately 25% of your portfolio in bonds (50 years old – 25 = 25%). This will protect a decent percentage of your investments from any major stock market downturn, but even so, you still have 10-15 years to absorb the next down market (which *will* happen in that time frame) and then ride the recovery wave back up as the market rebounds.

As many people can grudgingly attest to, if you were planning on retiring in 2009 and all of your investments were in stocks, then the 50% stock market decline caused you to delay your retirement by several years. For example, if during that time you had 40% of your investments in bonds (65 years old – 25 = 40%), which would have limited the loss in your portfolio, then your delay in retirement would have not nearly been as significant. Of course, hindsight is always 20/20, so again it simply goes back to your risk tolerance, and whether or not you plan on retiring at a specific age.

In terms of which "type" of bonds you should invest in, the simplest strategy would be to use a "total bond market index fund." This spreads your money across all different types of bonds and thus gives you the overall average of the entire bond market. Anything more specific than this will require more in-depth knowledge and is obviously beyond the scope of this book!

## BOND THEORY TWO

Now it should be noted that there are many financial experts that simply do not recommend bonds at all. They feel it limits your portfolio from earning a maximum return year after year. While this is true, and I personally tend to agree with it, this approach should only be taken by individuals who have a very high risk tolerance, and who plan on continuing to invest well beyond the classic retirement age of 65.

For someone who continues to invest throughout their lives, they will "always" have 10-15 years of investing ahead of them to ride out any down turns in the stock market that may (and will) occur. If you introduce bonds into your investment mix, you can expect that your overall investment portfolio will not produce nearly as high a return. For example, if a portfolio WITHOUT bonds is expected to generate an annual rate of return of 10%-12%, then a portfolio WITH bonds (depending on how much) can be expected to generate an annual rate of return of only 6%-8%.

# CHAPTER 16 – MUTUAL FUNDS

The next topic we will discuss concerning the stock market is the most important in terms of your investment strategy.

Mutual funds, as briefly mentioned before, are a pre-arranged group of individual company stocks. Each mutual fund is overseen and managed by a professional investment company or an individual within that company. There are thousands of different mutual funds available to invest in, and they can range from funds with only a handful of companies, to funds that are comprised of thousands of companies. The group of companies contained within a mutual fund is based on the specific type/category of the mutual fund. For example, there are funds that are invested in technology companies, industrial companies, medical companies, financial companies, real estate companies, foreign companies, small companies, large companies, and the list goes on and on.

When investing in a mutual fund, you automatically get the benefit of "diversification." This mean that your investment money is spread among various companies in order to minimize the risk of a single company having a substantial decrease in value and thus causing a large percentage of your overall investment portfolio to decrease. Based on this brief explanation, the average investor should have the vast majority (if not all!) of their long-term investment dollars in mutual funds as opposed to single stocks.

Before we go any further, it is important to point out that there can in fact be fees and expenses associated with mutual funds. Without going into great detail, the fees and expenses include purchase fees (paid when buying the mutual fund), exchange fees (paid when transferring money to another mutual fund), redemption fees (paid when selling a mutual fund) and management/service/account fees or 12b-1 fees (paid to help cover the costs of the mutual fund company). All of the fees associated with a mutual fund are often referred to as the "expense ratio" or "expense fee." This fee alone typically ranges from 0.5% - 1.5%, and it is paid directly to the mutual fund company that is overseeing or "managing" the fund.

Lastly, there are expenses called "loads" that also can be associated with mutual funds. These expenses are basically "commission" that is paid to your broker or financial advisor. These can be a "front-end" load (paid up front when you purchase a mutual fund) or a "back-end" load (paid when you sell the mutual fund), and can range from 2.0%-7.0%.

Well, what do all of these fees actually mean for you, the investor? Let's say you are investing $1,000 into a particular mutual fund. The fund you choose has an expense ratio/fee of 1.5%, and a front-end sales load of 3.5%. Without getting too mathematical, what you are essentially doing is giving up 5.0% (or $50) of your investment right away, and thus essentially only investing $950. This may not seem like much when only dealing with a one-time $1,000 investment. However, make no mistake about it, if you were to instead include that $50 for each $1,000 investment you make, then your money would grow substantially larger in the long run. So, in order to make up for these losses, a particular mutual fund with high fees must out-perform other mutual funds that do not have these fees (or have smaller fees). To justify these fees, many mutual fund managers will make the claim (whether true or not) that they can in fact out-perform the average mutual fund by giving you a higher rate of return. I say all of this to simply educate you on what you should be aware of prior to making the decision to invest in a particular mutual fund.

Now without getting too in-depth, mutual funds are overseen by fund managers (as I mentioned earlier), and are referred to as "actively managed funds." In other words, the list of individual stocks that make up a mutual fund is constantly analyzed (i.e. bought and sold within the fund) by the fund managers in order to get the best returns possible. This process of actively managing a group of stocks within a mutual fund has the potential to produce higher than average returns, yet historically only a fraction of mutual funds have done so.

According to historical data analyses (Ferri 2007 & Vanguard 2011), each year only 37% of these actively managed mutual funds beat the average stock market return. Over the span of five years, this percentage drops to 25%. Over ten years, it is down to 15%. Over twenty-five years, it is only 5%, and over fifty years, it is a mere 1%.

The point of the statistics above is that actively managed mutual funds have a low chance of beating the stock market as a whole year after year. Because of this, wouldn't you rather be invested in a type of mutual fund that *matches* the stock market's return? Well, the good news is that something like this does in fact exist, and that something is called an "index fund."

# CHAPTER 17 – INDEX FUNDS

Let me introduce you to the world of "index funds." Index funds are actually types of mutual funds, but instead of being actively managed by an individual or company, they are set up to match (as closely as possible) the entire stock market, or a particular portion it. In other words, ALL index funds are types of mutual funds, but NOT ALL mutual funds are index funds. Again, most mutual funds are actively managed and the stocks inside of them are bought and sold on a regular basis. Conversely, the stocks inside of index funds are not regularly bought and sold, but instead they are essentially kept the same in order to match a particular portion of the stock market. Because of this, index funds have extremely low fees associated with them.

Index funds come in all "shapes and sizes," and careful consideration must be taken when choosing an index fund. The first advantage of an index fund is that the associated fees are extremely low. The only fee associated with index funds is the expense ratio, and this fee generally ranges from 0.05% - 0.50%. If index funds are purchased by the investor themselves, then there will be no sales charge or commission (load) to pay!

The second advantage of index funds is that they can "match" the return of the entire stock market, or any specific area, as mentioned previously. The most common index funds are set up to match large-cap stocks, mid-cap stocks, small-cap stocks and international stocks.

Large-cap stocks are basically the largest companies in the stock market in terms of financial volume. The two primary large-cap index funds are S&P 500 index funds and Total Stock Market index funds. S&P 500 index funds invest your money in essentially all of the 500 largest publically traded companies in the U.S. (which make up the S&P 500 list). Total Stock Market index funds invest your money in the vast majority of all available stocks in the stock market and are *weighted* by company size/value. This means that the majority of the money in these funds is actually invested in the 500 companies that make up the S&P 500, thus the Total Stock Market index fund and the S&P 500 index fund are extremely similar in their overall growth.

The "mid-cap" and "small-cap" index funds contain the vast majority of companies that are considered to be mid-sized (companies with market capitalization ranging from $2-$10 billion) and small-sized (companies with market capitalizations ranging from $100 million to $2 billion), respectively. The international index fund contains the vast majority of companies located outside of the U.S.

There are also index funds that mirror certain categories of the bond market, or the entire bond market as a whole, which can be utilized when you reach your later years of investing (as discussed previously).

With such low expenses, index funds allow you to own large portions of the stock market without the inherent risks that are associated with actively-managed mutual funds (which are constantly buying and selling stocks, thus are more likely to produce lower returns than the overall market itself).

# CHAPTER 18 – STOCK MARKET SUMMARY

Okay, now that we have covered the basics of the stock market, it is imperative that you understand exactly what it is that you are investing in before you actually carry out any investment strategy. Even though I personally believe in investing in the stock market, you must understand it for yourself and be willing to accept the inherent risks that are involved.

In addition, there is one additional piece of information that you must take to heart. That is this: before you invest a single dollar, you must believe that the stock market as a whole will continue to increase over time, regardless of how it performs over one day, one week, one month, or even one year. The only tried and true way to grow your investments in the stock market is to consistently invest your money and then not take one dollar out until you are ready to use it in retirement. The only reason people ever lose money in the stock market is because they sell their investments (take their money out) when the market is decreasing. In case you did not know, there will ALWAYS be periods of time where the stock market goes down. However, in the history of the stock market, there has never been a time where the market did not subsequently increase and make up for any loss that might have occurred, and then ultimately reach higher levels than where it was previously.

In 2008-2009, the "Great Recession" hit the stock market, and as a whole, the market decreased by about 50%. This is something that has only happened one other time in history (the Great Depression of the late 1920s-early 1930s). The misconception with this was the feeling that investors "LOST 50% of their money" during the 2008 crash. This is incorrect. The only people who "lost money" were the people that sold their shares (or took their money out) due to fear. In fact, if you kept your money exactly where it was, then not only have you recovered everything that was lost in 2008, but your total investment has now (2014) gained over 15% on top of what you had before. For example, if you had $100,000 invested in 2008, you saw the total "value" of your investments drop all the way down below $50,000 by early 2009. If you had done nothing and just kept it where it was, then the value today (2014) would be over $115,000. This type of swing is very unlikely to happen again in your lifetime, but if it does, you need to be mentally prepared to ride it out and not panic! A more likely scenario is to see the market decline by 10%-20% over the course of a year or two, only to rebound in full and produce an additional increase of over 10% in the subsequent few years. If you can ride out this wave, which may last 3-4 years, then in the long run you will come out on top.

# CHAPTER 19 – TYPES OF INVESTMENT ACCOUNTS

Before we move on to the specifics on what your investment plan should look like, let me briefly explain the types of accounts that you are going to be opening to "house" all of your retirement money.

## 401(k) or 403(b)

If you are an employee of a company that offers a "retirement plan," then this will likely be a 401(k) or a 403(b). First off, the only difference between these two plans is that a 403(b) is for employees of non-profit organizations (charity, religious organization, hospital, public school system, etc.). Beyond that, they function in the exact same manner, with a few exceptions. For the rest of this book, I will only refer to a 401(k), but realize that if you are an employee of a non-profit or public institution, then I am referring to a 403(b) in your case.

Because 401(k) plans are often misunderstood, let's briefly define what they are. A 401(k) plan is basically a house in which your investments live. You cannot "buy" a 401(k), but rather you contribute your money to a 401(k) plan offered by your employer. That money is then invested into stocks, bonds, mutual funds, etc. In other words, your money is not "invested in a 401(k)," but instead it is housed in a 401(k), and then you decide how and where it is invested. I should mention that the company you work for chooses which types of investments are available within their 401(k) plan, and thus you, the employee, can be limited as to which stocks and mutual funds you can invest in. You can get the list of investment options from your Human Resources department or employee benefits office. If you are wondering which options (stocks, bonds, mutual funds and index funds) you should actually use *within* your 401(k), I will give you my recommendations in Chapter 21.

There is one more important topic to discuss about 401(k) plans which is often overlooked or misunderstood. Many companies currently offer what is called a "401(k) Match" or "Employer Match" as part of their 401(k) plan. This is the single greatest benefit that any employer can offer you to help you in your long-term wealth accumulation. The most common 401(k) match plan is to match 100% of what you contribute, up to 3% of your annual salary. In simple terms, if you make $50,000 and contribute 3% of your salary (or $1,500) into the company 401(k) plan, then your employer will automatically match 100% of that and deposit an additional $1,500 into your account. In essence, that is an automatic and instant 100% return on your investment! No matter what the percentage is, if you are offered a 401(k) match, then you should be contributing the maximum amount that your company will match. Rarely in life does "free money" exist, but this is one of those situations, so please do not pass it up!

An alternative to a 401(k) match would be a "profit-sharing plan." What this means is that your employer makes a discretionary deposit of money in your retirement account on your behalf. Some employers choose to calculate their profit sharing contribution based on company profits or the achievement of company goals. However, it is important to remember that the employer can choose when and how much to contribute. This plan actually does not require you to contribute any of your own money in order to qualify, but rather your employer does it automatically on your behalf. There are many variations to this plan, so make sure to contact your company HR department to get all of the specifics.

As we move on, we must also discuss the tax advantages of a 401(k) plan. When you contribute money to a 401(k), you are allowed to do so with "pre-tax" dollars, and therefore you do not have to pay taxes on this money. In other words, if you contribute $1,000 to your 401(k), then you are allowed to deduct $1,000 from your annual income when determining your taxes at the end of the year. For example, if your income for the year is $50,000, and you contribute $5,000 in your company 401(k) plan, then you only have to pay taxes on $45,000.

Instead of paying taxes now on the money that you contribute to your 401(k), you defer those taxes until you take that money out at retirement, and then pay the taxes at that point. (Note: this tax-deduction ONLY applies to the money that you contribute out of your own money/paycheck, and not on money that is "matched" or contributed by your company.) This, of course, can be an advantage or a disadvantage, depending on what your current tax bracket is and how large you expect your 401(k) to be when you retire. If you are concerned about this, then you should certainly seek the advice a certified public accountant or tax professional.

As of 2016, the maximum amount you are allowed to contribute to a 401(k) plan is $18,000 ($24,000 if you are 50 years or older). Obviously, this is a very large amount, and depending on how much your annual income is, this may or may not be attainable. However, regardless of your annual income, you should absolutely take full advantage of a company match, if offered.

**Traditional IRA**

A Traditional IRA (Individual Retirement Account) is an account that any individual can contribute to, regardless if they have a company 401(k) or not. As long as you have taxable compensation (income) or self-employment income, then you can contribute to an IRA (although you cannot contribute more than the total income reported on your tax return). You can simply go to your local bank or investment company and open your own Traditional IRA anytime you want, regardless of your employment status.

The two main differences between a Traditional IRA and a 401(k) plan are 1) within an IRA you are limited to a maximum contribution of $5,500 per year ($6,500 if you are 50 years or older), and 2) within an IRA you are allowed to invest your money into any investment category you desire (i.e. stocks, bonds, mutual funds, index funds, etc.). At the same time, a Traditional IRA is normally treated the same as a 401(k) in terms of getting a tax deduction up-front, but having to pay taxes on it later when you withdraw your money during retirement. If you (or your spouse) are covered by an employer-sponsored retirement plan and your income exceeds certain levels, then you may not be able to deduct your entire contribution at the end of the year. For example, if you are single and your adjusted gross income is over $71,000 for 2016, you will not receive a tax deduction for your Traditional IRA contribution if you are covered by a retirement plan at work. To determine if this applies to your situation, you should seek the advice a certified public accountant or tax professional.

When withdrawing your money from a Traditional IRA, you will need to wait until you are at least 59 ½ years old in order to avoid a 10% penalty. (If you were unable to deduct your Traditional IRA contribution, then the earnings are the only taxable portion when withdrawn.) There are a few exceptions to this rule, so please consult with a tax professional before making any withdrawals.

## Roth IRA

A Roth IRA is exactly the same as a Traditional IRA (including contribution limits), yet with one major difference. With a Roth IRA, you do not get a tax deduction on the contributions you make, but instead, this money grows completely tax-free, and thus you will not have to pay any taxes when you take it out during retirement. This potentially can be an amazing advantage in the long run, especially if you have amassed a substantial amount of money in your Roth IRA! The one caveat to this is that there is an income limit on who can contribute to a Roth IRA. In 2016, if you are filing your taxes as "Single," then your Modified Adjusted Gross Income (MAGI) must be less than $117,000. If you are "Married, Filing Jointly," then your MAGI must be less than $184,000. If your income is above these levels, then you are not allowed to contribute to a Roth IRA, and instead have to use the Traditional IRA.

**NOTE:** There is a "phase out range" of income that is slightly higher than the amounts listed, so if you make within $10,000 over those limits, then you still may be able to contribute a lesser amount to a Roth IRA. Please consult a tax professional to determine if you qualify.

In terms of withdrawing your money from a Roth IRA, there are a few rules that must be followed in order to avoid paying a 10% penalty. Just like the Traditional IRA, you must wait until you are at least 59 ½ years old. At the same time, you must wait at least 5 years from the time you contribute any money before you can make a withdrawal, even if you are over the age of 59 ½ . The one major caveat to these two rules is that any money that you actually contributed yourself can be withdrawn at any time without penalty. The 10% penalty only applies to any earnings or interest that has accumulated.

All IRA contributions are completely separate from 401(k) or 403(b) contributions, so you can in fact contribute to both at the same time, as long as you abide by the separate contribution limits imposed by each. This means that you can contribute the full $18,000 per year into the 401(k) and also contribute the full $5,500 into an IRA.

## Roth 401(k)

The Roth 401(k) acts just like the Roth IRA. However, this can only be offered through an employer. The tax advantages are exactly the same in that you are contributing "after-tax" dollars, and thus you do not get a tax deduction at the end of the year. The money in a Roth 401(k) grows tax-free, and you will not have to pay taxes on the money when you take it out during retirement. Like a Roth IRA, there are guidelines to follow in order to avoid a 10% penalty on early withdrawals, as previously mentioned.

The major advantage to the Roth 401(k), is that it abides by the same contribution limits as the traditional 401(k). This means that you can contribute up to $18,000 per year if you are under 50 years of age, or up to $24,000 if you are 50 years of age or older.

## "Back Door" Roth Conversion

I have one final piece of information that needs to be mentioned. For those of you who happen to be ineligible to contribute directly into a Roth IRA because of your income (earning more than $116,000 for a "single" individual, or $183,000 for "married, filing jointly"), please make note of this: the current tax code (as of this writing in 2014) actually allows for a Roth Conversion (or a "Back Door" Roth Conversion). This means that any money that is currently invested within a Traditional IRA (or other tax-deductible IRAs) can be converted to a Roth IRA each year. However, in doing so, the total amount of money converted is then considered as "additional earned income" and taxed as ordinary income. Because this money has already been given the tax advantage when it was contributed to the Traditional IRA (i.e. not taxed), it now becomes a taxable amount in order to be converted to a Roth IRA.

Because this option is so new, and quite frankly may not be around for very much longer, there are several nuances that require the advice and assistance of a tax professional to ensure that this conversion is done properly. With that being said, this is seemingly an amazing opportunity for high-income earners to convert a certain percentage of their Traditional IRA money over to a Roth IRA, and thus enjoy the long-term tax-free growth that previously was not afforded to them. I strongly urge you to consider this if you are able to handle the increased tax bill that will certainly accompany this conversion.

In addition to the types of accounts and plans discussed above, there are several other less-commonly utilized options for business owners and the self-employed (such as the SIMPLE IRA, 457 Plan, etc.). Please consult with a tax professional to discuss all of your options and determine which one would be best for your situation. The purpose of this chapter was to make you aware of the different types of accounts that are available for your retirement investing, based upon your employment status. It was not meant to give or to replace the advice of tax and accounting professionals.

**NOTE:** If you ARE NOT self-employed or own your own business, then the remainder of this chapter will not apply to you. However, if this is something you plan to pursue in the future, then I encourage you to read on, so that at least you will know what other investing options are available.

### SEP IRA

A SEP IRA stands for Simplified Employee Pension Plan, and essentially acts like a 401(k) plan for small business employers and their employees (if applicable). As a self-employed individual, whether or not you have employees working for you, you are allowed to invest into a SEP IRA and a Traditional/Roth IRA.

If you are a small business owner or self-employed, and you would like to make additional retirement investments beyond the $5,500 limit imposed by Traditional IRAs and Roth IRAs, then the

SEP IRA is likely your best option. The SEP IRA is fully tax-deductible (in that regard, it acts like a 401(k) or Traditional IRA) and has very generous contribution limits. In 2016, you are allowed to contribute up to $53,000 or 20% of your income, whichever is *smaller.* Unless you are making over $265,000 per year, the 20% limitation is what you will need to abide by.

**NOTE:** For the self-employed, this percentage is actually closer to 18.6% based on your adjusted net profit after the deduction for self-employment tax. Please consult a tax-professional to assess your particular situation, especially if you are planning on contributing over 15% of your income.

The other important stipulation to note is that if you have employees (that meet the IRS definition of an employee), then whatever percentage of your own salary that you contribute to your SEP IRA, you must also contribute the exact same percentage of your employees' salaries into their SEP IRAs. This essentially becomes a "forced benefit" and therefore an additional business expense, so this must be discussed with your tax advisor or accountant when considering a SEP IRA.

If a SEP IRA does in fact make sense for your situation, then it is a great way to maximize the amount of money you can invest while giving you additional tax deductions.

**SOLO 401(k)**

Another potential option for someone who is self-employed (with no full-time employees other than a spouse) is the SOLO 401(k). This is very similar to the general 401(k) and SEP IRA in terms of tax deductions. It does, however, require a higher level of oversight compared to the SEP IRA in terms of paperwork and record-keeping.

The SOLO 401(k) allows a self-employed individual to contribute up to $18,000 per year (or up to $24,000 if 50 years or older) in what is deemed "salary deferral." So as long as you make at least $18,000 in salary for the year, you can contribute up to that maximum (which is different from the SEP IRA). Further, you are allowed to contribute an additional 20% of your net profit, as long as the total yearly contribution does not exceed $53,000.

Additionally, the SOLO 401(k) does allow you to designate it as a SOLO Roth 401(k) if you choose to, regardless of your annual income. If you were to designate it as a SOLO Roth 401(k), then you would not get the immediate tax deduction, but instead, the money would grow tax-free and therefore not be taxed when you withdraw it.

When deciding between a SOLO 401(k) and a SEP IRA as part of your investment strategy, it is essential to discuss these (and all other) options with a tax professional.

# CHAPTER 20 – CREATING AN INVESTMENT PLAN

No matter what age you are, you must decide how much money you will need in order to retire comfortably (meaning that you no longer have to work for a paycheck, but instead you can live on the income that your retirement accounts produce). The underlying purpose of this book is to give you a roadmap that enables you to retire as a millionaire, no matter what your annual income was during your working years. Therefore, for anyone 15-39 years old, this number should be a minimum of $2,000,000 ($2 million). Based on estimated inflation, in 25 years from now, the buying power of $2 million will be roughly the same as $1 million today. This would in fact make you a millionaire (or technically a multi-millionaire) when you retire, which should be attainable for anyone under the age of 40!

**NOTE:** If you are between 40-49 years old in 2014, then your goal should be roughly $1.5 million, and if you are 50+, then you goal should be roughly $1 million. Of course, these numbers can vary greatly depending on how much you currently have saved and what you expect your retirement to look like.

In order to reach these goals (which to some people may seem unattainable or light-years away), you must systematically invest a minimum amount based on 1) your age and 2) how much you currently have saved for retirement. I call this your "MIN" or Minimum/Monthly Investment Number. If you are fortunate enough to be reading this book in your teens or 20s, then you can likely invest as little as $100-$150 per month, and still achieve the multi-million dollar retirement goal. If you are starting in your 30s, then this number will likely need to be $200-$400 per month, depending on how much you currently have in your retirement account. If you are starting in your 40s or beyond, then you are looking at $500-$1,000 per month, if not higher.

**How do you determine your MIN or Minimum/Monthly Investment Number?**

The charts in this chapter show you a year-by-year (Table 1) or a quarter-by-quarter (Table 2) breakdown of how much retirement money you should currently have based on how old you are, and how much you should be investing on an ongoing monthly basis if you intend to reach the multi-millionaire level ($2 million or more). This is a system I devised called the "Russell 2.0 Plan," which essentially puts you on track to accumulate $2.0 million or more by the time you reach 65 years old. As you will see by reading through the table, there is an incremental increase in the amount that you need to invest over time to reach the $2 million goal. The reason I came up with this system is because I have found that it is relatively easy to start out investing a small amount in your 20s (i.e. $100 per month), and then systematically increase that number by $100 per month as you enter each new decade of life. Please be aware that the amount of money you invest in your 20s has the greatest impact on your long-term wealth accumulation because this money has the most time to grow due to the wonders of compound interest. (For an alternative to this method [Appendix A], you can instead invest only $150 per month from age 21 to age 65, and you will actually reach the same $2 million goal!)

It is very simple to follow. Starting on Page 91 (Table 1), look in column 1 to find your current age. Then look in column 2 for the Minimum/Monthly Investment Number (MIN) that you should be investing. Finally, look in column 3 to see where you should be at in terms of your total retirement account savings. If you have the amount from column 3 currently invested in your IRA or 401(k) and are contributing a monthly amount equal to or greater than the corresponding MIN in column 2, then you are on track for a multi-millionaire retirement! For example, if you are 27 years old, then you should have at least $12,585 in your retirement account before your next birthday, and you should currently be investing at least $100 per month. If each one of those conditions is met, then job well done! If your total retirement account is lower than the goal amount in column 3, then you will need to raise you MIN by as much as you can until you reach your target balance for your current age.

**Author's Encouragement**

Even though the tables (in this chapter and in Appendix A) show incredible long-term growth with relatively small amounts of monthly investments (anywhere from $100-$400), I would like to encourage you not to *limit* yourself to these amounts.

With a Traditional IRA or Roth IRA, you are currently allowed to invest just over $450 per month. If you work for a company that offers a 401(k) or you are self-employed, you are allowed to invest substantially more than this on a monthly basis!

Depending on your specific situation, it is always advisable to increase your monthly investing by as much as you can handle (ideally up to 10-15% of your income). The more you can invest and the younger you are, the greater the likelihood that you will attain and even surpass the example numbers used in this book.

The following investment tables use an estimated 10.8% yearly return, and may vary greatly depending on the variability of the stock market.

# Table 1 – Russell 2.0 Investment Strategy (Yearly)

| Age | Monthly | Balance |
|-----|---------|---------|
| 21 | $100 | $1,272 |
| 22 | $100 | $2,689 |
| 23 | $100 | $4,267 |
| 24 | $100 | $6,024 |
| 25 | $100 | $7,980 |
| 26 | $100 | $10,159 |
| 27 | $100 | $12,585 |
| 28 | $100 | $15,286 |
| 29 | $100 | $18,293 |
| 30 | $200 | $22,915 |
| 31 | $200 | $28,061 |
| 32 | $200 | $33,792 |
| 33 | $200 | $40,173 |
| 34 | $200 | $47,278 |
| 35 | $200 | $55,189 |
| 36 | $200 | $63,999 |
| 37 | $200 | $73,809 |
| 38 | $200 | $84,732 |
| 39 | $200 | $96,895 |
| 40 | $300 | $111,711 |
| 41 | $300 | $128,210 |
| 42 | $300 | $146,580 |
| 43 | $300 | $167,036 |
| 44 | $300 | $189,814 |
| 45 | $300 | $215,178 |
| 46 | $300 | $243,420 |
| 47 | $300 | $274,869 |
| 48 | $300 | $309,887 |
| 49 | $300 | $348,880 |

| Age | Monthly | Balance |
|---|---|---|
| 50 | $400 | $393,571 |
| 51 | $400 | $443,336 |
| 52 | $400 | $498,749 |
| 53 | $400 | $560,452 |
| 54 | $400 | $629,159 |
| 55 | $400 | $705,665 |
| 56 | $400 | $790,856 |
| 57 | $400 | $885,716 |
| 58 | $400 | $991,343 |
| 59 | $400 | $1,108,961 |
| 60 | $400 | $1,239,929 |
| 61 | $400 | $1,385,763 |
| 62 | $400 | $1,548,151 |
| 63 | $400 | $1,728,971 |
| 64 | $400 | $1,930,317 |
| 65 | $400 | $2,154,517 |

For those of you who would like to track your retirement savings more often than once per year, I have also put together a chart broken down by quarter (starting on the next page) so that you can track your progress four times per year. The quarterly numbers use an estimated 2.7% return per quarter.

# Table 2 – Russell 2.0 Investment Strategy (Quarterly)

| Age - Quarter | Monthly | Balance | Age - Quarter | Monthly | Balance |
|---|---|---|---|---|---|
| 21 - Q1 | $100 | $305 | 29 - Q4 | $100 | $17,895 |
| 21 - Q2 | $100 | $613 | 30 - Q1 | $200 | $18,978 |
| 21 - Q3 | $100 | $930 | 30 - Q2 | $200 | $20,091 |
| 21 - Q4 | $100 | $1,255 | 30 - Q3 | $200 | $21,233 |
| 22 - Q1 | $100 | $1,589 | 30 - Q4 | $200 | $22,407 |
| 22 - Q2 | $100 | $1,932 | 31 - Q1 | $200 | $23,612 |
| 22 - Q3 | $100 | $2,284 | 31 - Q2 | $200 | $24,849 |
| 22 - Q4 | $100 | $2,646 | 31 - Q3 | $200 | $26,120 |
| 23 - Q1 | $100 | $3,017 | 31 - Q4 | $200 | $27,425 |
| 23 - Q2 | $100 | $3,398 | 32 - Q1 | $200 | $28,766 |
| 23 - Q3 | $100 | $3,790 | 32 - Q2 | $200 | $30,143 |
| 23 - Q4 | $100 | $4,193 | 32 - Q3 | $200 | $31,556 |
| 24 - Q1 | $100 | $4,606 | 32 - Q4 | $200 | $33,008 |
| 24 - Q2 | $100 | $5,030 | 33 - Q1 | $200 | $34,500 |
| 24 - Q3 | $100 | $5,466 | 33 - Q2 | $200 | $36,031 |
| 24 - Q4 | $100 | $5,914 | 33 - Q3 | $200 | $37,604 |
| 25 - Q1 | $100 | $6,373 | 33 - Q4 | $200 | $39,219 |
| 25 - Q2 | $100 | $6,845 | 34 - Q1 | $200 | $40,878 |
| 25 - Q3 | $100 | $7,330 | 34 - Q2 | $200 | $42,582 |
| 25 - Q4 | $100 | $7,828 | 34 - Q3 | $200 | $44,332 |
| 26 - Q1 | $100 | $8,339 | 34 - Q4 | $200 | $46,129 |
| 26 - Q2 | $100 | $8,865 | 35 - Q1 | $200 | $47,974 |
| 26 - Q3 | $100 | $9,404 | 35 - Q2 | $200 | $49,869 |
| 26 - Q4 | $100 | $9,958 | 35 - Q3 | $200 | $51,816 |
| 27 - Q1 | $100 | $10,527 | 35 - Q4 | $200 | $53,815 |
| 27 - Q2 | $100 | $11,111 | 36 - Q1 | $200 | $55,868 |
| 27 - Q3 | $100 | $11,711 | 36 - Q2 | $200 | $57,976 |
| 27 - Q4 | $100 | $12,327 | 36 - Q3 | $200 | $60,142 |
| 28 - Q1 | $100 | $12,960 | 36 - Q4 | $200 | $62,366 |
| 28 - Q2 | $100 | $13,610 | 37 - Q1 | $200 | $64,650 |
| 28 - Q3 | $100 | $14,278 | 37 - Q2 | $200 | $66,995 |
| 28 - Q4 | $100 | $14,963 | 37 - Q3 | $200 | $69,404 |
| 29 - Q1 | $100 | $15,667 | 37 - Q4 | $200 | $71,878 |
| 29 - Q2 | $100 | $16,390 | 38 - Q1 | $200 | $74,419 |
| 29 - Q3 | $100 | $17,133 | 38 - Q2 | $200 | $77,028 |

| Age - Quarter | Monthly | Balance | Age - Quarter | Monthly | Balance |
|---|---|---|---|---|---|
| 38 - Q3 | $200 | $79,708 | 47 - Q4 | $300 | $265,884 |
| 38 - Q4 | $200 | $82,460 | 48 - Q1 | $300 | $273,963 |
| 39 - Q1 | $200 | $85,286 | 48 - Q2 | $300 | $282,260 |
| 39 - Q2 | $200 | $88,189 | 48 - Q3 | $300 | $290,781 |
| 39 - Q3 | $200 | $91,170 | 48 - Q4 | $300 | $299,532 |
| 39 - Q4 | $200 | $94,232 | 49 - Q1 | $300 | $308,520 |
| 40 - Q1 | $300 | $97,676 | 49 - Q2 | $300 | $317,750 |
| 40 - Q2 | $300 | $101,213 | 49 - Q3 | $300 | $327,229 |
| 40 - Q3 | $300 | $104,846 | 49 - Q4 | $300 | $336,964 |
| 40 - Q4 | $300 | $108,577 | 50 - Q1 | $400 | $347,262 |
| 41 - Q1 | $300 | $112,409 | 50 - Q2 | $400 | $357,838 |
| 41 - Q2 | $300 | $116,344 | 50 - Q3 | $400 | $368,700 |
| 41 - Q3 | $300 | $120,385 | 50 - Q4 | $400 | $379,855 |
| 41 - Q4 | $300 | $124,535 | 51 - Q1 | $400 | $391,311 |
| 42 - Q1 | $300 | $128,798 | 51 - Q4 | $400 | $427,569 |
| 42 - Q2 | $300 | $133,175 | 52 - Q1 | $400 | $440,313 |
| 42 - Q3 | $300 | $137,671 | 52 - Q2 | $400 | $453,402 |
| 42 - Q4 | $300 | $142,288 | 52 - Q3 | $400 | $466,843 |
| 43 - Q1 | $300 | $147,030 | 52 - Q4 | $400 | $480,648 |
| 43 - Q2 | $300 | $151,900 | 53 - Q1 | $400 | $494,826 |
| 43 - Q3 | $300 | $156,901 | 53 - Q2 | $400 | $509,386 |
| 43 - Q4 | $300 | $162,037 | 53 - Q3 | $400 | $524,340 |
| 44 - Q1 | $300 | $167,312 | 53 - Q4 | $400 | $539,697 |
| 44 - Q2 | $300 | $172,730 | 54 - Q1 | $400 | $555,469 |
| 44 - Q3 | $300 | $178,294 | 54 - Q2 | $400 | $571,666 |
| 44 - Q4 | $300 | $184,008 | 54 - Q3 | $400 | $588,301 |
| 45 - Q1 | $300 | $189,876 | 54 - Q4 | $400 | $605,385 |
| 45 - Q2 | $300 | $195,902 | 55 - Q1 | $400 | $622,931 |
| 45 - Q3 | $300 | $202,092 | 55 - Q2 | $400 | $640,950 |
| 45 - Q4 | $300 | $208,448 | 55 - Q3 | $400 | $659,456 |
| 46 - Q1 | $300 | $214,976 | 55 - Q4 | $400 | $678,461 |
| 46 - Q2 | $300 | $221,681 | 56 - Q1 | $400 | $697,979 |
| 46 - Q3 | $300 | $228,566 | 56 - Q2 | $400 | $718,025 |
| 46 - Q4 | $300 | $235,638 | 56 - Q3 | $400 | $738,611 |
| 47 - Q1 | $300 | $242,900 | 56 - Q4 | $400 | $759,754 |
| 47 - Q2 | $300 | $250,358 | 57 - Q1 | $400 | $781,467 |
| 47 - Q3 | $300 | $258,018 | 57 - Q2 | $400 | $803,767 |

| Age - Quarter | Monthly | Balance | | Age - Quarter | Monthly | Balance |
|---|---|---|---|---|---|---|
| 57 - Q3 | $400 | $826,669 | | 62 - Q1 | $400 | $1,362,713 |
| 57 - Q4 | $400 | $850,189 | | 62 - Q2 | $400 | $1,400,706 |
| 58 - Q1 | $400 | $874,344 | | 62 - Q3 | $400 | $1,452,448 |
| 58 - Q2 | $400 | $899,151 | | 62 - Q4 | $400 | $1,479,798 |
| 58 - Q3 | $400 | $924,628 | | 63 - Q1 | $400 | $1,520,952 |
| 58 - Q4 | $400 | $950,793 | | 63 - Q2 | $400 | $1,563,218 |
| 59 - Q1 | $400 | $977,665 | | 63 - Q3 | $400 | $1,606,625 |
| 59 - Q2 | $400 | $1,005,262 | | 63 - Q4 | $400 | $1,651,204 |
| 59 - Q3 | $400 | $1,033,604 | | 64 - Q1 | $400 | $1,696,986 |
| 59 - Q4 | $400 | $1,062,711 | | 64 - Q2 | $400 | $1,744,005 |
| 60 - Q1 | $400 | $1,092,604 | | 64 - Q3 | $400 | $1,792,293 |
| 60 - Q2 | $400 | $1,123,305 | | 64 - Q4 | $400 | $1,841,885 |
| 60 - Q3 | $400 | $1,154,834 | | 65 - Q1 | $400 | $1,892,816 |
| 60 - Q4 | $400 | $1,187,214 | | 65 - Q2 | $400 | $1,945,122 |
| 61 - Q1 | $400 | $1,220,469 | | 65 - Q3 | $400 | $1,998,840 |
| 61 - Q2 | $400 | $1,254,622 | | 65 - Q4 | $400 | $2,054,009 |
| 61 - Q3 | $400 | $1,289,697 | | | | |
| 61 - Q4 | $400 | $1,325,718 | | | | |

**NOTE:** "Q1" = January-March, "Q2" = April-June, "Q3" = July-September, "Q4" = October-December. The dollar amount in the third column represents the expected total on the last day of the quarter.

**Special Consideration:** Although both of the charts above represent the growth of a *single* IRA, the same numbers can be used as benchmarks for a married couple. In fact, for a married couple, your goal should be for your combined monthly investment total to equal or exceed the numbers in the charts above. But whether you are single or married, $2.0 million will still make for a very comfortable and luxurious retirement!

# CHAPTER 21 – THE SPECIFICS OF YOUR INVESTMENT PLAN

Now that you are familiar with the different retirement accounts (IRA, 401(k), etc.) and the amount of money you should be investing monthly, we will next discuss which specific accounts you should use and what type of funds you should invest in. Below is a comprehensive, step-by-step list that should answer all of your specific questions.

**What type of account?**

1) If you work for a company that offers a 401(k) match, then this is a no-brainer. Most of the time, companies will match 100% of the first 3% (or maybe 50% of the first 6%) of your salary that you contribute. In other words, this is essentially giving you an automatic and incredible return on your money of either 100% or 50%, respectively! Whatever your MIN (minimum/monthly investment number) is, make sure that YOU are contributing this number, and count your employer match as a "bonus"! If you reach the maximum percentage that your company will match, and your MIN is still higher, or you simply want to invest more, then the remaining dollars each month should go into a Roth IRA. If you are ineligible for a Roth IRA due to your income, then you can either contribute to a Traditional IRA, or simply continue to contribute to your 401(k). Remember, as of 2016 you can contribute up to $18,000 a year to your 401(k), or $1,500 per month!

2) If you do not work for a company that matches your contributions, then your first step is to open a Roth IRA. Remember, although you do not get a tax deduction at the end of the year, you will never have to pay taxes on this money in the future when you pull it out for retirement. If you are ineligible for a Roth IRA, then open a Traditional IRA. Whatever your MIN is, then simply contribute *at least* this amount directly into your IRA each month. Remember, if you are under 50 years old, you can contribute a maximum of $5,500 per year (or $458 per month). If you are over 50 years old, then you are allowed to contribute up to $6,500 per year (or $541 per month).

**NOTE:** All of the numbers mentioned in #1 and #2 are PER INDIVIDUAL, so if you are married, you can actually invest that amount twice.

**Where to invest?**

Below you will find the asset allocation strategy (where to specifically invest your money within your 401(k) or IRA) that I recommend for every person reading this book. Not only is it my recommendation, but it is also the recommendation of billionaire investor Warren Buffet and multi-millionaire investor (and founder of Vanguard) John "Jack" Bogle.

First off, in order to achieve the highest annual return on your investment (ROI), you must be invested in the stock market (also referred to as "equities"). If you remember from previous chapters, this is done by either investing in individual stocks, mutual funds, or index funds. In my opinion, and in the opinion of many investment experts, your entire investment portfolio should consist of index funds. This minimizes the overall costs that you have to pay on your investments, and thus maximizes the long-term, compounding growth of your money.

From all of the information that I have gathered, there are only 4 categories of index funds that you need to consider: 1) Large Cap Index Fund, 2) Small Cap Index Fund, 3) International Index Fund and 4) Bond Index Fund (if you choose to include bonds in your portfolio – see Chapter 15).

Investment firms such as Charles Schwab, Fidelity, Vanguard, etc. generally offer each of these index funds. If the particular company that you invest with (or your 401(k) plan) does not have a classic index fund for each of the 4 categories listed above, then you may decide to use a traditional mutual fund, but please be very careful to choose one that has the absolute lowest cost and no associated fees! An investment advisor at each of these firms will help you choose the appropriate fund with the lowest cost (and this simple advice should be free of charge).

So, how should my money be allocated (spread out) among each of these index funds? Great question! Besides the amount of money that you invest, how you allocate your money is the most important variable that will determine how large your investment portfolio will grow! There are two ways to answer this question: 1) based on your risk tolerance, and 2) based on your age. The charts on the following pages will give you a suggested breakdown of how much of your money should be invested in each of the different types of index funds.

**NOTE:** The following percentages are estimates. If you decide to use the "Age – 25 = Bond %" formula, then your percentages will differ slightly.

**For those who decide to include Bonds in their portfolio**

If based on risk tolerance:

| Very Conservative | 60% Large Cap<br>40% Bond |
|---|---|
| Conservative | 60% Large Cap<br>30% Bond<br>5% Small Cap<br>5% International |
| Moderate | 60% Large Cap<br>20% Bond<br>10% Small Cap<br>10% International |
| Aggressive | 50% Large Cap<br>25% Small Cap<br>15% International<br>10% Bond |
| Very Aggressive | 40% Large Cap<br>40% Small Cap<br>20% International |

If based on age:

| Under 21 | 100% Large Cap |
|---|---|
| 21-29 | 50% Large Cap<br>30% Small Cap<br>20% International |
| 30-39 | 50% Large Cap<br>25% Small Cap<br>15% International<br>10% Bond |
| 40-49 | 60% Large Cap<br>20% Bond<br>10% Small Cap<br>10% International |
| 50-59 | 60% Large Cap<br>30% Bond,<br>5% Small Cap<br>5% International |
| 60 and over | 60% Large Cap<br>40% Bond |

**For those who decide NOT to include Bonds in their portfolio**

If based on risk tolerance:

| Very Conservative | 100% Large Cap |
|---|---|
| Conservative | 80% Large Cap<br>10% Small Cap<br>10% International |
| Moderate | 60% Large Cap<br>20% Small Cap<br>20% International |
| Aggressive | 50% Large Cap<br>30% Small Cap<br>20% International |
| Very Aggressive | 40% Large Cap<br>40% Small Cap<br>20% International |

If based on age:

| Under 21 | 100% Large Cap |
|---|---|
| 21-29 | 40% Large Cap<br>40% Small Cap<br>20% International |
| 30-39 | 50% Large Cap<br>30% Small Cap<br>20% International |
| 40-49 | 60% Large Cap<br>20% Small Cap<br>20% International |
| 50-59 | 70% Large Cap<br>15% Small Cap<br>15% International |
| 60 and over | 80% Large Cap<br>10% Small Cap<br>10% International |

**NOTE:** When referring to a "Large Cap Index Fund," this can be either a "Total Stock Market Index Fund" or an "S&P 500 Index Fund," as they are both cap-weighted index funds and thus match each other very closely.

Again, there is no hard and fast rule for the percentage breakdown that you choose. However, before you decide on how your investments are allocated, you must understand what you are investing in, the risk involved (i.e. how much you are willing to take), and the amount of time you have before you need the money. The younger you are, then the more time you have to ride out the ups and downs of the stock market. Conversely, the older you are, the greater you would feel the effect of a 20% decrease in the market since you have a limited amount of time to wait for it to rebound!

We discussed this earlier, but I will mention it again here. Once you have decided which specific funds your money is going to be invested in, you MUST have this money withdrawn automatically from your checking or savings account! If you do not have your investing done automatically, then there is a very high chance that it simply will not happen (i.e. you will likely forget to do it). With any investment company, or through the payroll department at your workplace, you can have your money automatically withdrawn, and then directly invested into the funds that you choose. Remember, since we are viewing this as a "required monthly expense," then having it automated just like your utility bill or internet bill is imperative. Trust me on this one!

If I can give you one more critical piece of advice, it would be this: please do not hesitate or be ashamed to ask for help! Most investment companies will offer consultation free of charge. Simply tell them what you would like your investment strategy to be (based on the previous charts, with any modifications that you feel comfortable with), and they will gladly help you get it set up and choose the appropriate funds. As I mentioned earlier, you should plan to have each of the three categories (Large, Small and International) captured within an index fund! Of course, just because you have an account with Charles Schwab, doesn't mean that you can't have some of your money invested in a Vanguard index fund, and vice versa. Simply stay strong in your belief that it is best to have the lowest cost index fund possible, which should have fees that are less than .40% for each of these categories (and less than .10% for the large-cap index funds). If the consultant tries to dissuade you from using all index funds, then politely but sternly either walk away, or ask to speak with someone else!

If a personal financial advisor is a better fit for your personality (someone who invests/manages your money for you, following your direction of course, and looks after your accounts), then please make sure that this arrangement is set up on a fee-only basis. In other words, pay your financial advisor by the hour or half-hour to help you with your accounts (once a year is more than enough), as opposed to paying a commission upwards of 4% or 5% on all of the money you invest. This is simply not needed because you are using index funds, automatically investing a fixed amount every month, and following a very strict "buy-and-hold" strategy (meaning not selling any of your investments EVER, until you need the money in retirement). A high-quality financial advisor may charge upwards of $100-$200 per hour, but once a sound strategy is in place and automated, it should not have to be addressed for at least 5-10 years (other than the basic, annual "check-up").

I want to stress the fact that I am not "against" financial advisors. They can actually be (and often are) very helpful in keeping you on track with your goals. They also typically help oversee other financial products such as life insurance, disability insurance, 529 college savings plans, etc. If you are the type of person that may be tempted to pull your money out when you see the stock market going down, or someone that may be tempted to use the money in your investment account for something like furniture, vacations or a new car, then you are absolutely a perfect candidate for having a paid financial advisor on your "team."

One final word on this subject: you should make it a habit to either check monthly or quarterly that the money being taken out of your checking account is accurately being invested the way you have intended. Any reputable investment company should always be investing your money exactly how you have set it up, but it is your responsibility to confirm this!

Lastly, for those of you who are doing all of your investing through a work-sponsored plan, such as a 401(k), you will find that you are very limited in your options when it comes to index funds. In fact, it is very common to find that the only index fund your company offers is an S&P 500 index fund. Don't worry! In this case, I would encourage you to put the majority of your money into the S&P 500 index fund (anywhere from 50%-80%), and then split the remaining percentage between a small-cap fund and an international fund. I would choose these last two funds based on two criteria: 1) overall fees for the fund, and 2) long-term track record of the fund. You should be able to find both of these funds with less than a 1.00% associated fee, and also a track record of at least 10 years with an annual rate of return close to 10% (if not higher!). If both of these criteria are not able to be met, then I would strongly consider either not investing in them or limiting your percentage to 10%. By default, this would mean that you would be putting more money into the S&P 500 index fund and I have no problem with that whatsoever! In fact, it you simply want to put 100% into the S&P 500 index fund because all of the other mutual fund options have high fees and poor track records, then I would fully support that decision. This course of action will likely turn out to be the best decision over the long haul!

# CHAPTER 22 – PROTECTING YOUR WEALTH

One of the biggest and most tragic mistakes that people make is not creating a solid layer of protection around their financial future. Again, for the purpose of this book, I will briefly discuss the five major areas of protection that EVERY SINGLE PERSON should have in place (with very few exceptions, which will be mentioned).

## Health Insurance

Let me say right off the bat, if you are reading this book, then it is imperative that you have health insurance. Medical bills are one of the most common causes for personal bankruptcy in America. Regardless of who you are and how much you make, having a health insurance policy in place is essential. In fact, recent laws have been enacted that allow all people, regardless of past medical history or income level, to have health insurance.

For some reason, many people have the mentality of "nothing serious will ever happen to me." Whether or not that ends up being reality, the fact of the matter is that one slip and fall, one car accident or one sudden illness can create a bill worth tens of thousands of dollars, and in some cases hundreds of thousands of dollars. What most people fail to realize is this: the number one reason why you have health insurance is to safeguard yourself against any financially catastrophic medical event. At the very minimum, a high-deductible plan should be in place for you and your family (especially if you have children!), that limits your out-of-pocket expenses if something major were to occur.

If your job offers health insurance, of which most do if you are eligible, then that is almost always going to be the most cost effective plan. If you are not covered through a work plan, then you must enroll yourself and your immediate family (if applicable) into a private insurance plan.

Whether it is through work or in the private market, there are several different types and aspects of health insurance that you must be knowledgeable about. When determining which health insurance policy that is right for you, one must take into account the deductible that is associated with the plan, and also the percentage that is covered once the deductible is met.

First off, the deductible is basically the up-front cost that you are personally liable for before the insurance coverage kicks in. This can range from $0 to $10,000 or more. The higher the deductible, the lower the monthly or annual premium is going to be.

With some high deductible plans, you have the option to open up a Health Savings Account (HSA). This account allows you to put money in tax-free (it becomes a tax-deductible contribution), and as long as it is used for "qualified medical expenses," then it is also tax-free when you make withdrawals. Further, the money that you place into an HSA can then be invested in a wide variety of investment options, including mutual funds and index funds. Also, any growth on this money is completely tax free when used to pay medical expenses. This is an excellent place to save and invest so that you will have money available if you ever have to use your high deductible insurance coverage. (The maximum yearly amount you can contribute into your HSA for 2016 is $3,350 for an individual plan or $6,750 for a family plan).

The second factor that you must be aware of is the percentage of coverage that you are responsible for AFTER your deductible has been met (called co-insurance). It is very common for companies to offer plans in which you are responsible for 10%-20% of your medical costs even after you have paid your deductible. However, this does usually come with a yearly "out-of-pocket" maximum. Once this yearly maximum has been reached, your insurance company will then cover 100% of all additional expenses for that calendar year. Of course, you can get a policy in which you have 0% financial responsibility after your deductible is met (in other words your insurance company will cover 100% of medical costs after you reach your deductible), but these plans often cost substantially more in terms of monthly/annual premiums.

If you have a plan that requires you to be responsible for 10% or 20% of your medical costs after your deductible is met, then it becomes your responsibility to know the total dollar amount of your yearly "out-of-pocket" maximum, and have that exact amount added to your emergency fund.

Here is an example. Let's say you have health insurance with a $1,000 deductible plus a 20% co-insurance responsibility (after the deductible is met). If something were to happen in which your medical expenses for the year reached $16,000, then you are going to be left with a $4,000 bill. To break that down, the first $1,000 is your responsibility in the form of your deductible. After that is paid, your insurance company will then cover 80% of the $15,000 balance, which is equal to $12,000. The remaining 20%, or $3,000, will be your responsibility, and if you don't have this money saved, then it becomes your $4,000 debt ($1,000 + $3,000)! This is a very common cause of debt in America today, but if you have this all accounted for in your personal finance plan from the very beginning, it will not become an area of stress in your life, nor will it derail your plan for long-term wealth accumulation!

## Disability Insurance

One area that is very often overlooked is insuring oneself in the event of a short-term or long-term disability. Current statistics show that for 20-year olds in America, 1 out of every 4 (25%) will experience some sort of disabling illness or injury before age 67 that will prevent them from earning an income for an extended period of time [2013 Social Security fact sheet]. Further, one in seven working individuals (regardless of age) will experience a disability before they retire that will last for at least 5 years. With all of your planning, budgeting, saving and investing, the basic foundational assumption is that your income will continue to come in month after month. But what happens if you experience some sort of injury or illness that prevents your income from coming in for 6 months, 12 months or even 60 months? This is exactly why you should have disability insurance. For most people, going without their monthly income for any duration of time would be detrimental to their overall financial plan.

There are two basic types of disability insurance: "short-term," which provides supplemental income for 3-6 months (this range can vary), and "long-term," which provides supplemental income for 5 years, 10 years or all the way until age 65. In basic terms, if you are unable to earn an income because of an injury or illness, disability insurance then pays you a predetermined, fixed amount every month while you are "disabled" for whatever duration your policy states. In addition, these disability payments are typically tax-free, thus you will only need to replace 50%-75% of your monthly *gross* income.

Often times the most affordable way to obtain disability insurance is through your employer, but just like health insurance, there is a large private market where you can obtain this insurance on your own. As a quick rule of thumb, an individual should carry disability insurance in the amount of at least 50% of their monthly income (or at least the amount of money it takes to cover their minimum monthly expenses). This policy should include at least five years of disability coverage. If you are married and have children, you should highly consider a policy that covers you for at least 10 years or through age 65.

# Life Insurance

Life insurance is very similar to disability insurance in terms of the financial implications, yet with one major difference: life insurance provides income replacement in the event that the policy holder passes away. If there is anyone in your life that depends on your income to live (i.e. spouse, children, etc.), then having a life insurance policy is essential. The basic recommendation is to have a policy in force that would pay your surviving dependents an amount equal to 10 times your annual income. For example, if you make $50,000 per year, then you should have a life insurance policy in the amount of $500,000 for your family to live off of. This number generally works because, if invested correctly, your loved ones should be able to live year after year on the 10% interest that it earns (i.e. $50,000) without decreasing the principal amount (i.e. $500,000).

There are basically two different types of life insurance policies: "whole-life" and "term-life." (Now there are many variations of whole-life policies, also referred to as "permanent," but for the purposes of this book I will generally lump them all under the same heading). "Whole-life" insurance is essentially a policy that is in effect for your entire life. It stays with you until you die, and then pays the "face value" (or death benefit amount) to your survivors once you pass away. These policies require you to make a large monthly payment, and they use your money to pay policy fees as well as save/invest some of your money within the policy. One advantage of these policies is that they remain in effect for your entire life, and then leave a lump sum to your heirs once you pass away. Another advantage is that it "forces" you to save and invest a portion of your money every month in case you were to need it down the road. One major disadvantage is that the monthly payments are extremely high and part of that is lost in order to pay policy costs and fees. Another disadvantage is that most of the time these policies keep any money that has accrued within the policy and only payout the face value when you pass away.

The alternate option is called "term-life" insurance. These policies are very simple in that they also have a specific face value (or death benefit amount) and they only remain in force for a fixed number of years, based on the type of policy you choose. This duration can be anywhere from 5 years to 50 years, although the most common range is from 10 years to 30 years. As an example, you can have a 20-year, $500,000 "term-life" policy in place that will pay your loved ones the full amount if you were to pass away within 20 years of the policy start date. Once the 20-year period elapses, the policy is no longer in affect. The main advantage of a "term-life" policy is that it has an extremely low monthly cost. For a $500,000 policy, assuming the individual is 25 years old and in overall good health, a "term-life" policy would cost somewhere in the neighborhood of $35.00 per month. For the same valued "whole-life" policy, this would cost about $235.00 per month (these are simply estimations and may vary greatly).

Because we know that $200 per month can drastically grow over time when invested wisely, the monthly savings of the "term-life" policy compared to the "whole-life" policy causes a vast difference in the long-term values of each. By using a 20-year, "term-life" policy from age 25 to 45 and investing the additional $200 per month into a Roth IRA (for example), your investment would reach an astonishing $170,000 at the end of the 20-year policy (assuming a 10.8% annual return). If you continue to invest the difference (which is now $235 because you are no longer paying the $35 for the "term-life" policy) from age 45 to 60, the total amount of your investment becomes $960,000, which nearly doubles the face value of the "whole-life" policy. The only scenario in which a "whole-life" policy makes sense is if you already have it in place, and you now have a medical condition which prevents you from getting a new policy.

However, if you are a relatively healthy individual, then every year that you live past 60 greatly enhances the benefits of using the "term-life" strategy. In fact, if you were to continue to invest that $235 per month from age 60 to 75, the total value of your investments would be over $4,000,000. Now which would you rather leave to your loved ones if you passed away at age 75: a "whole-life" policy worth $500,000 plus any potential money that has grown within the policy (limited by the associated costs and fees), or an investment account worth $4,000,000?

**NOTE**: I understand that many people, namely insurance agents, will argue the specific numbers in the paragraph above. I will concede that there may be certain types of "whole-life" products that might actually accumulate an additional $500,000 or more in value above the $500,000 death benefit if kept until age 75, making it a $1,000,000+ product. But even with below average returns on index funds for the next 50 years, the total of your $200 or $235 monthly investment would likely grow to no less than $3,000,000, thus still making the difference in this comparison a whopping $2,000,000! I should also point out that the math above is based on the assumption that this decision is being made by a 25 year old. If an older individual is doing a similar cost analysis, the math would be quite different.

With these simple comparisons in mind, it is my opinion, and one that is shared by a number of financial gurus around the country, that a "term-life" policy is clearly the way to go. By minimizing your monthly cost and investing the amount that you would save by not having a "whole-life" policy, you can then see how easy it is to increase your overall net worth by a substantial amount. To go one step further, there are so many hidden fees and rules associated with "whole-life" policies (whether variable, universal, hybrid, etc.), that they should be avoided at all costs until you have a 7-figure net worth and can afford the extremely high costs (and even then I would strongly advise against it).

In closing, if you currently have a "whole-life" policy, then you should cancel the policy as soon as possible and take any cash value (surrender value) that may be there (please talk with your tax advisor, NOT your insurance agent, to determine any tax implications). Of course you should have your "term-life" policy in place BEFORE you do this, and then add the total amount of money that you will save each month to your overall monthly investment. (If you are unable to obtain a "term-life" policy due to health reasons, then you will be forced to keep your "whole-life" policy.) If you have only had your "whole-life" policy for a few months or years, then you will likely be told that you are throwing away a good chunk of money by doing this and that you might as well keep it. Yes, it is true that you may be throwing away thousands of dollars if it is a recent policy, but I firmly believe that you will be throwing away many hundreds of thousands of dollars if you keep that "whole-life" policy for another 30, 40 or 50 years. The choice is yours!

**Last Will and Testament**

Simply put, a Will is the only way that you can be certain that your money is protected from being taken by or distributed to people against your wishes. It is amazing how complicated things can get in terms of dividing and distributing your assets if you do not have a clear plan in writing. This ranges from the government (through unwarranted taxes) to former, estranged or distant family members. If you follow the principles and guidelines laid out in this book and achieve a 7-figure net worth, a Will is essential for dictating how and where your wealth will be distributed so that these very situations can be avoided.

Most people think that this is a very complicated and expensive procedure that only "rich" people should do. Nothing could be further from the truth! A Will can be created by using an online, legal document website for less than $50 per person (it is imperative that each individual have their own Will, even if they are married). It also allows for you to appoint an individual(s) to oversee the management and distribution of your assets. Often times when you are leaving anything of substantial value to minors or young adults, you may want to have some or all of your assets transferred to a "trust," which can then be distributed to the individual in certain increments and at certain times.

Without a Will, it is possible for your assets to be tied up in the court systems for months, if not years, before your loved ones can prove their right of ownership. This undue stress and frustration is certainly not something you want to leave with your family and loved ones.

**Identity Theft Protection**

Although you may be under the impression that identity theft is over-exaggerated as well as over-reported, it is still very much a threat to your overall wealth. For as little as $10 - $25 per month, you can be enrolled in a quality identity theft protection program that will work with you to resolve your issue and recoup any lost or stolen money. There are even some companies that will assign a case worker to you so that your actual time spent on restoring your identity is limited as much as possible. Even with the protection offered nowadays through your bank, credit card company or debit card company, attempting to restore your identity can easily amount to dozens of hours over the span of each month. Depending on the value of your time, this risk may simply not be worth taking.

It should be noted that there are several ID protection services out there that are more "scam" than anything else. It is imperative that you do your research and choose a company with a long track record and one with positive reviews and actual testimonials. This may in fact be with your bank or financial institution, but it may also be with a national, third party organization. Whichever you decide to go with, make sure you get in writing which specific services they will and will not provide. Having good protection in place can give you peace of mind, and at the same time save you dozens of hours and thousands or tens of thousands of dollars!

## Bonus – Children's Educational Fund

I do want to highly recommend one more area that is often overlooked or undervalued when creating a financial plan: the area of college education. Currently (in 2014), a four-year college degree can range anywhere from $20,000 to $200,000 when tuition, fees, books and housing are all accounted for. This range varies greatly depending on whether your child attends a public vs. private university, or stays in-state vs. out of state. If you are reading this book with young children, then you can astonishingly expect this range to at least double over the next 15-20 years.

Without proper planning, one of the following four scenarios will almost certainly occur: 1) you will use a significant portion of your retirement savings to pay for your child's education in order to lessen the burden on them, 2) you will end up taking out a loan for your child, of which causes you to go into debt and thus limits your investing potential, 3) your child will take out a student loan and then be burdened by student loan payments for 5, 10 or even 20 years after graduation, or 4) if going into debt is not an option, then your child will simply not be able to attend college.

Obviously none of these scenarios are what we would call a "good option," but they are the only options that millions of American families face each and every year. On the other hand, a fifth option would be to start investing for college while your child is at a very young age, thus allowing compound interest to wondrously increase the amount of money available for your child when they are ready for college.

The two best options available for this are called the Educational Savings Plan (ESP) and the 529 Plan. They both allow your investment to grow tax-free over time, and as long as it is used for qualified educational expenses (i.e. tuition, books, room and board, etc.), then the money is distributed tax-free as well. The ESP has a lower annual limit on how much you can invest ($2,000 per year as of 2014), but it also gives you complete control over where to invest your money. 529 Plans allow for up to $14,000 per year per contributor (meaning a husband and wife could each contribute $14,000 per year per kid, without penalty or taxation), and are managed by every individual state. You should note that you do not need to invest in your own state's 529 Plan. However, there are a few states that offer incentives (tax deduction, etc.) for their residents to invest in their home state's 529 Plan. The other important variable to consider when choosing a 529 Plan is whether it allows you to have complete control over where your money is invested (which most do not). You only want to be in a plan where you can choose your own mutual funds (ideally the index funds that we discussed earlier) and are free to re-allocate your investments at least once per year with no penalty.

Funding your child's future education is absolutely a personal choice, but one that I highly recommend. For example, if you invest $100 per month from the time your child is born until they turn 18 years old, then their college account will likely be close to $70,000. No matter what the amount, any money that you can save for your child by the time they turn 18 will limit (if not eliminate) the amount of out of pocket expenses they will have to pay for school (which usually manifests itself in the form of student loan debt). Further, saving money early on will reduce or eliminate the possibility of feeling compelled to use some of your personal retirement money to "help out" your child, or the possibility of you being asked to do so once your child realizes that they do not have the money to pay for college.

# CHAPTER 23 – AGE BY AGE RECAP

Now that you have just read through an entire book full of valuable financial information, let's review all of the take-home points, and most importantly, answer the all-important question "what am I supposed to do now?"

We will go through each age bracket and recap each step for you to follow on your quest for financial independence!

Please read each of these sections (especially the ones beyond your age so that you know what to expect in the future), but remember that the one that matches your age is the one you should be following at this phase of your life. Many phases have considerable overlap.

**Under 21 Years Old**

1) Congratulate yourself for reading this book at such a young age and for acquiring the life-changing knowledge that most people twice or even three times your age can only wish they had learned earlier!

2) Do whatever it takes to stay out of consumer debt! This includes student loans! Whether that means going to a more affordable state or community college, or working 20-30 hours per week WHILE taking classes, you will be so thankful that you enter your 20s without tens of thousands (or hundreds of thousands!) of dollars in student loans. If you have already accumulated student loans, then make it a point not to take out anymore!

3) Open up a savings account and save at least $1,000. If you own your own car, which most of you probably do, then I would go ahead and bump this up to $2,000. This will take some work, but everything in life will automatically feel different when you know that you have a few thousand dollars in the bank in case of an emergency!

4) Pay off any debt that you might already have! This is likely to be credit card debt. If so, you will want to break the habit RIGHT NOW of buying things you simply cannot afford or do not have the money for.

5) If you have a job and are paying taxes on an earned income, then you should open up a Roth IRA. You can do this online or in person, and it can be through your local bank or investment company (Charles Schwab, Fidelity, Vanguard, etc.). You can contribute up to $5,500 per year, or up to the total amount of income that you earned (or will earn) this year, whichever is smaller. There may be an initial investment minimum or a monthly minimum to meet, so talk to the company that you are going to use to find out the specifics. Whatever amount you can invest by the time you reach 21 years old will ultimately be worth more than you can possibly imagine by the time you retire!

6) In general, you should be giving 10%, saving 10%, investing 10% and living on (enjoying!) the rest. If you have a specific savings goal in mind (house, car, wedding, etc.), then you should increase your savings percentage and learn to live on even less!

## 21-29 Years Old

1) Open up a savings account and save at least $1,000. Depending where you are in this age range, and what you own (car, home, etc.), you may want this to be slightly higher. If you are married with or without children, then I would definitely recommend this to be in the $2,000-$3,000 range. This account is simply for any immediate emergencies that arise in your life (new tires, car repairs, home repairs, medical bills, etc.). This is NOT a vacation or shopping spree fund!

2) Get rid of ALL consumer debt in your life, other than your primary home mortgage (if you have one). For some, this may be less than $1,000. For others, it may be over $50,000 (it could even be several times higher if you have amassed a large amount of student loan debt). If this seems impossible, let me encourage you that nothing is impossible if you put your mind to it and if you have a burning desire to accomplish it! In recommending Dave Ramsey's debt snowball process, simply list all of your debts, smallest to largest (regardless of the interest rates), pay the minimum on each, and then throw any extra money you have on the smallest one. Once it is paid off, you then take the amount you were paying on that debt, and apply it to the next smallest debt. With each debt that is eliminated, the amount of money that you can put towards the next debt becomes even greater. Hence, the snowball effect! Please note that this step may take several years to complete.

3) Your next step is to have a fully-funded emergency fund. This means you should eventually save 25%-50% of your annual income in a cash account for big emergencies. In other words, this total should be roughly 6 months of household expenses. If your combined household income is $40,000, then you will want to start saving until you have $10,000-$20,000 in a cash account that you do not touch unless an emergency arises or you reach retirement!

4) Saving for a house is also important in this phase of life. Your goal should be to save enough money for a 10%-20% down payment, with a mortgage payment that is no higher than 25% of your monthly net (take-home) income. If you follow this advice, then you will almost never have to worry about your house payment becoming a cause of stress in your life! Far too many people spend half (or more!) of their monthly income on a house payment, and they wonder why they have financial stress or why they cannot afford to save and invest for their future.

5) If you haven't begun investing for retirement, then you need to start today! Talk to your employer about their retirement plan, and/or contact an investment company about opening a Roth IRA (through Fidelity, Charles Schwab, Vanguard, etc.). As you have read in previous chapters, your retirement investing should look like this:

 - At a very minimum you should be investing $100 per month (see Russell 2.0 Chart on pages 91-92), although your ultimate goal should always be 10%-15% of your monthly income.

 - First, if your company offers a 401(k) match, then you should contribute up to the amount that qualifies for the match.

 - Next, contribute to a Roth IRA, up to $5,500 per year.

 - If you still have more money to invest, then go back to your company 401(k) and put the remainder there.

 - Refer to the Age and Risk Tolerance Tables (pages 99-100) to determine the allocation percentages you should be implementing with your investments.

6) If you are behind where you need to be on the Russell 2.0 Chart, then you will need to increase your investing (either monthly or in lump sums) for the short term until you reach the appropriate level.

7) If you have children, you should be investing a minimum of $100 per month, per child into a 529 Plan or Educational Savings Account. This will help reduce or even eliminate the "temptation" for your child to take out student loans for college.

8) Make sure you have a Will in place, as well as adequate health insurance, disability insurance and term life insurance (if you are married and/or have children).

## 30-39 Years Old

1) Open up a savings account and save at least $1,000. Depending where you are in this age range, and what you own (car, home, etc.), you may want this to be slightly higher. If you are married with or without children, then I would definitely recommend this to be in the $2,000-$3,000 range. This account is simply for any immediate emergencies that arise in your life (new tires, car repairs, home repairs, medical bills, etc.). This is NOT a vacation or shopping spree fund!

2) Get rid of ALL consumer debt in your life, other than your primary home mortgage (if you have one). For some, this may be less than $1,000. For others, it may be over $50,000. (It could even be several times higher if you are still paying off student loan debt or have things such as car loans, credit card debt, medical bills or a Home Equity Line of Credit [HELOC]). If this seems impossible, let me encourage you that nothing is impossible if you put your mind to it and if you have a burning desire to accomplish it! In recommending Dave Ramsey's debt snowball process, simply list all of your debts, smallest to largest (regardless of the interest rates), pay the minimum on each, and then throw any extra money you have on the smallest one. Once it is paid off, you then take the amount you were paying on that debt, and apply it to the next smallest debt. With each debt that is eliminated, the amount of money that you can put towards the next debt becomes even greater. Hence, the snowball effect! Please note that this step may take several years to complete.

3) Once your debt is gone (everything other than your primary home mortgage), then you need to start focusing on your emergency fund, investing for retirement and saving for college (if you have children).

**NOTE:** If you have yet to purchase your own home, please refer to #4 from the 21-29 year old section for guidelines.

4) For your emergency fund, you should have the goal of saving an amount equal to 25%-50% of your annual salary. This total should be roughly 6 months of household expenses. Once this account has been fully funded, you can stop saving and then increase the amount you invest and/or give. You could also add to your college savings or increase your house payments in order to pay it off sooner!

5) If you haven't begun investing for retirement, then you really need to kick it into high gear. Talk to your employer about their retirement plan, and/or contact an investment company about opening a Roth IRA (if you do not qualify due to a high income, then open a Traditional IRA). Refer to the Russell 2.0 Chart to see where you should be based upon you current age. As you have read in previous chapters, your retirement investing should look like this:

- At a very minimum you should be investing $200 per month (see Russell 2.0 Chart on pages 91-92), although your ultimate goal should always be 10%-15% of your monthly income.

- First, if your company offers a 401(k) match, then you should contribute up to the amount that qualifies for the match.

- Next, contribute to a Roth IRA, up to $5,500 per year. Be sure to check the income eligibility requirements. If you are over the limit, then open up a Traditional IRA and fund that.

- If you still have more money to invest, then go back to your company 401(k) and put the remainder there.

- Refer to the Age and Risk Tolerance Tables (pages 99-100) to determine the allocation percentages you should be implementing with your investments.

6) If you are behind where you need to be on the Russell 2.0 Chart, then you will need to increase your investing (either monthly or in large chunks) for the short term until you reach the appropriate level.

7) If you have children, you should be investing a minimum of $100 per month, per child into a 529 Plan or Educational Savings Account. This will help reduce or even eliminate the "temptation" for your child to take out student loans for college!

8) Make sure you have a Will in place, as well as adequate health insurance, disability insurance and term life insurance (if you are married and/or have children).

9) Once all of this is in place, you then want to start doing everything you can to pay off the balance of your home mortgage!

## 40-49 Years Old

1) Open up a savings account and save at least $1,000. Depending on where you are in this age range, and what you own (car, home, etc.), you may want this to be slightly higher. If you are married with or without children, then I would definitely recommend this to be in the $2,000-$3,000 range. This account is simply for any immediate emergencies that arise in your life (new tires, car repairs, home repairs, medical bills, etc.). This is NOT a vacation or shopping spree fund!

2) Get rid of ALL consumer debt in your life, other than your primary home mortgage (if you have one). For some, this may be less than $1,000. For others, it may be over $50,000. (It could even be several times higher if you are still paying off student loan debt or have things such as car loans, credit card debt, medical bills or a Home Equity Line of Credit [HELOC]). If this seems impossible, let me encourage you that nothing is impossible if you put your mind to it and if you have a burning desire to accomplish it! In recommending Dave Ramsey's debt snowball process, simply list all of your debts, smallest to largest (regardless of the interest rates), pay the minimum on each, and then throw any extra money you have on the smallest one. Once it is paid off, you then take the amount you were paying on that debt, and apply it to the next smallest debt. With each debt that is eliminated, the amount of money that you can put towards the next debt becomes even greater. Hence, the snowball effect! Please note that this step may take several years to complete.

3) Once your debt is gone (everything other than your primary home mortgage), then you need to start focusing on your emergency fund, investing for retirement and saving for college (if you have children).

4) For your emergency fund, you should have the goal of saving an amount equal to 25%-50% of your annual salary. This total should be roughly 6 months of household

expenses. Once this account has been fully funded, you can then stop saving and in turn increase the amount you invest and/or give. You could also add to your college savings or increase your house payments in order to pay it off sooner!

5) If you haven't begun investing for retirement, then you need to shift into emergency mode and do whatever it takes to invest as much as you can each and every month. Talk to your employer about their retirement plan, and/or contact an investment company about opening a Roth IRA (if you do not qualify due to a high income, then open a Traditional IRA). Refer to the Russell 2.0 Chart to see where you should be at based upon you current age. If you have just recently started saving for retirement, then you can reduce the goal numbers in the chart by 25%, which would put your retirement goal at $1.5 million. As you have read in previous chapters, your retirement investing should look like this:

- At a very minimum you should be investing $300 per month (see Russell 2.0 Chart on pages 91-92), although your ultimate goal should always be 10%-15% of your monthly income.

- First, if your company offers a 401(k) match, then you should contribute up to the amount that qualifies for the match.

- Next, contribute to a Roth IRA, up to $5,500 per year. Be sure to check the income eligibility requirements. If you are over the limit, then open up a Traditional IRA and fund that.

- If you still have more money to invest, then go back to your company 401(k) and put the remainder there.

- Refer to the Age and Risk Tolerance Tables (pages 99-100) to determine the allocation percentages you should be implementing with your investments.

6) If you are behind where you need to be on the Russell 2.0 Chart, then you will need to increase your investing (either monthly or in large chunks) for the short term until you reach the appropriate level.

7) If you have children, you should be investing a minimum of $150 per month, per child into a 529 Plan or Educational Savings Account (unless their college funding is already in place). This will help reduce or even eliminate the "temptation" for your child to take out student loans for college! If your children are teenagers and you are just starting to fund their college savings, then you will want to be VERY conservative with how you invest this money. You may even consider just using a high-yield savings account, bonds or CDs if you have less than 5 years before you will need to start withdrawing the funds.

8) Make sure you have a Will in place, as well as adequate health insurance, disability insurance and term life insurance (if you are married and/or have children).

9) Once all of this is in place, you then want to start doing everything you can to pay off the balance of your home mortgage!

## 50+ Years Old

1) Open up a savings account and save at least $1,000. Depending on where you are in this age range, and what you own (car, home, etc.), you may want this to be slightly higher. If you are married with or without children, then I would definitely recommend this to be in the $2,000-$3,000 range. This account is simply for any immediate emergencies that arise in your life (new tires, car repairs, home repairs, medical bills, etc.). This is NOT a vacation or shopping spree fund!

2) Get rid of ALL consumer debt in your life, other than your primary home mortgage (if you have one). For some, this may be less than $1,000. For others, it may be over $50,000. (It could even be several times higher if you are still paying off student loan debt or have things such as car loans, credit card debt, medical bills or a Home Equity Line of Credit [HELOC]). If this seems impossible, let me encourage you that nothing is impossible if you put your mind to it and if you have a burning desire to accomplish it! In recommending Dave Ramsey's debt snowball process, simply list all of your debts, smallest to largest (regardless of the interest rates), pay the minimum on each, and then throw any extra money you have on the smallest one. Once it is paid off, you then take the amount you were paying on that debt, and apply it to the next smallest debt. With each debt that is eliminated, the amount of money that you can put towards the next debt becomes even greater. Hence, the snowball effect! Please note that this step may take several years to complete.

3) Once your debt is gone (everything other than your primary home mortgage), then you need to start focusing on your emergency fund, investing for retirement and saving for college (if you have children).

4) For your emergency fund, you should have the goal of saving an amount equal to 25%-50% of your annual salary. This total should be roughly 6 months of household

expenses. Once this account has been fully funded, you should focus solely on maximizing your monthly investing!

5) If you haven't begun investing for retirement, then you need to shift to emergency mode and do whatever it takes to invest as much as you can each and every month. Talk to your employer about their retirement plan, and/or contact an investment company about opening a Roth IRA (if you do not qualify due to a high income, then open a Traditional IRA). If you refer to the Russell 2.0 Chart, it would be appropriate to cut each goal number in half since you are relatively close to retirement (if you are currently in your 50s, then it is safe to say that your minimum retirement goal should be between $750,000 and $1 million, as opposed to $2 million). As you have read in previous chapters, your retirement investing should look like this:

- At a very minimum you should be investing $400 per month (see Russell 2.0 Chart on pages 91-92), although your ultimate goal should always be 10%-15% of your monthly income.

- First, if your company offers a 401(k) match, then you should contribute up to the amount that qualifies for the match.

- Next, contribute to a Roth IRA, up to $6,500 per year. Be sure to check the income eligibility requirements. If you are over the limit, then open up a Traditional IRA and fund that.

- If you still have more money to invest, then go back to your company 401(k) and put the remainder there.

- Refer to the Age and Risk Tolerance Tables (pages 99-100) to determine the allocation percentages you should be implementing with your investment.

6) If you are behind where you need to be on the Russell 2.0 Chart (modified in half), then you will need to increase your investing (either monthly or in large chunks) for the short term until you reach the appropriate level.

7) Make sure you have a Will in place, as well as adequate health insurance, disability insurance and term life insurance (if you are married and/or have children).

8) Once all of this is in place, you then want to start doing everything you can to pay off the balance of your home mortgage early!

# CHAPTER 24 – FINAL MOTIVATION

Congratulations! You have now obtained what could equate to a multi-million dollar education on the topic of personal finance! As you let all of this information sink in, I want to encourage you to read through this book at least one more time so that you can really allow these concepts to go from your head to your heart.

To quote Dave Ramsey, "Personal finance is 80% behavior and 20% head knowledge." This means that just a small amount of financial knowledge is all you need if it is coupled with practical and consistent behavior. You can take all of this information that we have just discussed and memorize every detail, yet still end up completely broke in 10 years. How is that possible? Without a behavioral change that lines your thinking up with the ideals spelled out in this book, you are unlikely to ever achieve financial freedom. Even though you know that you need to spend less than you make, to pay yourself first by saving and investing, to establish a budget that you follow every month, and to remain consistent in your newly found attitude towards money, simply *knowing* all of this is not enough! Without actually waking up every day and applying these principles to your life, you will be in the same place financially year after year. Your day-to-day behavior when it comes to your money is absolutely vital if you want to achieve success in long-term wealth accumulation.

Regardless of where you came from and how you used to treat the topic of money and personal finance, I want to encourage you to make the change today and line your thinking up with the principles discussed in this book.

I realize that you may not agree with each and every detail discussed in this book, but that is not the point.

The point is to get you to start paying attention to what your finances are doing on a monthly basis.

The point is for you to understand the importance of giving, saving and investing in order to maximize your potential for long-term wealth accumulation.

The point is to change the way you think and feel about money, no matter how much you actually receive in the form of income, and to understand that you can become financially independent if you set your mind to it.

And finally, the point is to convince you that with a little foundational knowledge, along with the required consistent behavioral modifications, you can and will become an expert at MOTIVATING YOUR MONEY!

# SCENARIO #1:
## TWIN SIBLINGS

Johnny and Joanna are twin siblings, who throughout their lives both amassed very sizeable retirement accounts. However, they accomplished this feat in two very different manners. Let's examine the different paths they took to get to the place where they could comfortably retire at the age of 65.

*Johnny's Story:*

When Johnny was 18 years old, he attended a financial planning seminar that educated him on the very same topics found in this book. He learned that even with a relatively small amount of money invested every month for a long period of time, he could retire as a millionaire. The seminar taught him to budget his monthly expenses so that he would have extra money each month to invest for his future. Part of what he learned was to delay his short-term desires (immediate gratification of buying "stuff") in order to enhance his potential for long-term wealth accumulation.

After acquiring all of this financial knowledge, Johnny devised the following game plan: he would enjoy his college years and early 20s, and then when his career started to advance and he was ready to settle down and start a family, he would begin consistently and systematically investing every month into his Roth IRA.

So at 28 years old, Johnny was married, had a job that paid him $50,000 per year, and was ready to start investing. He opened up a Roth IRA and began contributing $200 every month (all into low-cost index funds). He set this up to automatically be withdrawn from his checking account and then invested into the funds he chose. His investment strategy was implemented from the day he turned 28 years old and stayed exactly the same until the day he turned 65. This equated to 37 years of investing $2,400 each year, for an out of pocket total of $88,800.

To Johnny's credit, this was an amazing display of dedication and consistency to be able to invest $200 each and every month for 37 years! Although the market fluctuated from year to year, he was never tempted to sell or "move" his investments around, and ultimately his portfolio averaged a 10.8% annual rate of return over the span of 37 years.

The day Johnny turned 65 years old, his retirement account had grown to a total of $1,070,000.

*Joanna's Story:*

Now Joanna happened to attend that very same seminar with Johnny back when she was 18 years old. She understood the importance of what was being taught, and just like her brother, she knew that this was something that she needed to do if she wanted to retire as a millionaire. However, being slightly better at math then Johnny was, Joanna also realized the incredible power of compounding interest, and really got excited knowing that she had over 45 years until she reached retirement. Because of this, Joanna devised her own game plan, which was slightly different than Johnny's.

Joanna decided that in order to take full advantage of compounding interest, she needed to start investing as soon as possible. Even though she only made $8,000 per year (working part-time during college), she decided to start investing right away. In order to maximize her long-term wealth accumulation, Joanna realized that this would require some sacrifice on her part, especially in terms of how she spent her money on a day to day basis. So the day she turned 19, Joanna opened up a Roth IRA and started contributing $200 every month. Just like her brother Johnny, she set this up to be automatically withdrawn from her checking account each month, and invested into low-cost index funds.

However, at the age of 28, after only 9 years of investing, life began putting pressure on Joanna's finances. The major factor was that Joanna had just given birth to her very own set of twins! This was also her third and fourth child! Being that her and her husband were making less than $45,000 per year, they came to the decision that they really needed the extra $200 each month, so they reluctantly stopped Joanna's automatic $200 monthly investment. In fact, they got so used to having this extra money that they never again invested a single dollar.

The day Joanna turned 65 years old, her retirement account had grown to a total of $1,627,000.

Wait a minute! Did that just say that Joanna had over $550,000 MORE in her account than her brother Johnny? I thought Johnny had consistently invested his $200 every month for 37 years! Joanna only invested her money for 9 years! How is this possible?

This is the power of compounding interest. Even though Joanna only invested for 9 years, her total at the end of those 9 years was roughly $36,000. Over the next 37 years, her money grew at an average of 10.8% each year, and even without adding another dollar to it, her total became over $1.6 million!

Just in case you were wondering, if Joanna had been able to continue her $200 per month investment all the way until age 65, her account would have grown to an astonishing $3,130,000! This would have been an additional $1.5 million, or almost twice the amount she actually ended up with!

# SCENARIO #2:
## THE SURGEON AND THE THERAPIST

Dr. John Back, M.D. is a 65 year-old spine surgeon who has been in private practice since the age of 33. His annual salary has been between $500,000 - $800,000 over the span of 32 years. Jane Stretch, PT is a 65 year-old physical therapist who specializes in post-operative spine patients. Jane began her physical therapy career at the age of 24, which was 8 years before Dr. Back started his career. Jane's annual salary has been between $40,000 - $65,000 over the span of 41 years. Both Jane and Dr. Back worked for the same medical group their entire careers, and ended up retiring the same year. Surprisingly, they both ended up with the exact same amount in their retirement account at the age of 65. Let's see how that happened!

*Dr. Back's story:*

Dr. Back and his wife raised their four children in a very affluent neighborhood. All four children went to private school which averaged $50,000 per year. Each of their children received a four-year college degree, with one becoming an M.D., one becoming an attorney, and the other two receiving their M.B.A. degrees. Dr. Back and his wife cash-flowed every degree that their children earned, which amounted to over $1.3 million over the course of 12 years. The Backs also bought brand new luxury vehicles every two years. They have always worn designer clothes, jewelry, watches and accessories, which easily averages $5,000 per month. They are members of a country club and a yacht club, which costs them $2,000 per month. And of course they own a yacht, worth over $500,000 (that they financed), of which requires over $4,000 per month in upkeep and fuel, not to mention the $3,000 monthly loan payment. They live in a $1.2 million home, and also own a $700,000 beach home. They financed both of these properties, which costs the Back family over $12,000 per month in mortgages and taxes. They also enjoy two exotic vacations a year, which easily costs them over $15,000 for each.

As you can see from this brief description, Dr. Back is an expert at spending and enjoying his money. With such an incredible salary coming in year after year, this lifestyle is easily maintained. However, with the enormous amount of money being earned and spent on a monthly basis, Dr. Back rarely contributes any money to his company's 401(k) plan. Since the age of 40, he has had a relatively small amount of money (in his case) that would be automatically invested on his behalf, but this only amounted to about $1,500 a month, or the equivalent of 3% of his monthly salary.

Over the past few years, he has realized that his dream of retiring in comfort is very much in jeopardy. On his 65th birthday, his entire retirement account was *only* $2.2 million. This may seem like a very large number, but consider this: Dr. Back has been used to earning (and spending) $50,000 per month. If he were to live off of the interest that his investments earn him each year (withdrawing a conservative 8% so as not to touch the principal balance), then his monthly income in retirement will end up being only $15,000 per month. Based on his real estate costs alone, Dr. Back and his wife will not be able to survive financially with this plan. They will be forced to sell their vacation home and their yacht, stop driving brand new cars, and drastically reduce their high consumption lifestyle. Then, and only then, will they be able to *comfortably* retire. If they cannot make these major lifestyle changes, then Dr. Back will be forced to work well into his 70s.

*Jane Stretch's story:*

Ms. Jane Stretch and her husband live a completely different lifestyle than that of Dr. Back and his family. The Stretch family also have four children, all of whom went to public school from kindergarten through college graduation. Jane had always believed in investing for her children's college education, and she had over $30,000 saved up in a college fund for each of her children. Since all four went to state universities, this was more than enough for all of their undergraduate expenses. The Stretch family lived very modestly, in a four bedroom home worth $200,000, of which they paid off before their oldest child graduated high school!

Jane and her husband always lived well below their means. They drove 4 year-old used cars, shopped on a budget, and never spent lavishly on any one single item or category. Jane's husband was a social worker, and therefore their combined annual salary ranged from $60,000 - $85,000. Even though they made anywhere from $5,000 - $7,000 each month, they always lived on less than they made each month, and diligently saved and invested the rest. When they were 30 years old, Jane and her husband started contributing a total of $500 per month into their Roth IRAs. By the time they reached age 65, Jane and her husband had an incredible $2.2 million. As you will recall, this is the same amount that Dr. Back had in his retirement account! Using the same 8% number previously mentioned, the Stretch family will now have a monthly income of $15,000 during retirement, which is more than double the income they had while working! This increase in income now allows them to travel as much as much as they would like, live a more lavish lifestyle, and give to others on a level that was never before possible!

# APPENDIX A

## Russell 2.0 Investment Strategy (Yearly) – Alternative

| Age | Monthly | Balance |
|-----|---------|---------|
| 21 | $150 | $1,908 |
| 22 | $150 | $4,034 |
| 23 | $150 | $6,401 |
| 24 | $150 | $9,036 |
| 25 | $150 | $11,971 |
| 26 | $150 | $15,238 |
| 27 | $150 | $18,877 |
| 28 | $150 | $22,929 |
| 29 | $150 | $27,440 |
| 30 | $150 | $32,464 |
| 31 | $150 | $38,058 |
| 32 | $150 | $44,287 |
| 33 | $150 | $51,222 |
| 34 | $150 | $58,946 |
| 35 | $150 | $67,545 |
| 36 | $150 | $77,121 |
| 37 | $150 | $87,784 |
| 38 | $150 | $99,658 |
| 39 | $150 | $112,879 |
| 40 | $150 | $127,600 |
| 41 | $150 | $143,993 |
| 42 | $150 | $162,247 |
| 43 | $150 | $182,572 |
| 44 | $150 | $205,205 |
| 45 | $150 | $230,406 |
| 46 | $150 | $258,469 |
| 47 | $150 | $289,716 |
| 48 | $150 | $324,511 |
| 49 | $150 | $363,255 |

| Age | Monthly | Balance |
|---|---|---|
| 50 | $150 | $406,397 |
| 51 | $150 | $454,435 |
| 52 | $150 | $507,927 |
| 53 | $150 | $567,491 |
| 54 | $150 | $633,815 |
| 55 | $150 | $707,668 |
| 56 | $150 | $789,905 |
| 57 | $150 | $881,475 |
| 58 | $150 | $983,440 |
| 59 | $150 | $1,096,979 |
| 60 | $150 | $1,223,406 |
| 61 | $150 | $1,364,183 |
| 62 | $150 | $1,520,940 |
| 63 | $150 | $1,695,490 |
| 64 | $150 | $1,889,854 |
| 65 | $150 | $2,106,279 |

# Russell 2.0 Investment Strategy (Quarterly) – Alternative

| Age - Quarter | Monthly | Balance | Age - Quarter | Monthly | Balance |
|---|---|---|---|---|---|
| 21 - Q1 | $150 | $458 | 29 - Q1 | $150 | $16,025 |
| 21 - Q2 | $150 | $770 | 29 - Q2 | $150 | $16,758 |
| 21 - Q3 | $150 | $1,091 | 29 - Q3 | $150 | $17,510 |
| 21 - Q4 | $150 | $1,420 | 29 - Q4 | $150 | $18,283 |
| 22 - Q1 | $150 | $1,759 | 30 - Q1 | $150 | $19,377 |
| 22 - Q2 | $150 | $2,106 | 30 - Q2 | $150 | $20,500 |
| 22 - Q3 | $150 | $2,463 | 30 - Q3 | $150 | $21,654 |
| 22 - Q4 | $150 | $2,830 | 30 - Q4 | $150 | $22,838 |
| 23 - Q1 | $150 | $3,206 | 31 - Q1 | $150 | $24,055 |
| 23 - Q2 | $150 | $3,593 | 31 - Q2 | $150 | $25,304 |
| 23 - Q3 | $150 | $3,990 | 31 - Q3 | $150 | $26,588 |
| 23 - Q4 | $150 | $4,397 | 31 - Q4 | $150 | $27,906 |
| 24 - Q1 | $150 | $4,816 | 32 - Q1 | $150 | $29,259 |
| 24 - Q2 | $150 | $5,246 | 32 - Q2 | $150 | $30,649 |
| 24 - Q3 | $150 | $5,688 | 32 - Q3 | $150 | $32,077 |
| 24 - Q4 | $150 | $6,141 | 32 - Q4 | $150 | $33,543 |
| 25 - Q1 | $150 | $6,607 | 33 - Q1 | $150 | $35,048 |
| 25 - Q2 | $150 | $7,086 | 33 - Q2 | $150 | $36,595 |
| 25 - Q3 | $150 | $7,577 | 33 - Q3 | $150 | $38,183 |
| 25 - Q4 | $150 | $8,081 | 33 - Q4 | $150 | $39,814 |
| 26 - Q1 | $150 | $8,600 | 34 - Q1 | $150 | $41,489 |
| 26 - Q2 | $150 | $9,132 | 34 - Q2 | $150 | $43,209 |
| 26 - Q3 | $150 | $9,678 | 34 - Q3 | $150 | $44,975 |
| 26 - Q4 | $150 | $10,240 | 34 - Q4 | $150 | $46,790 |
| 27 - Q1 | $150 | $10,816 | 35 - Q1 | $150 | $48,653 |
| 27 - Q2 | $150 | $11,408 | 35 - Q2 | $150 | $50,567 |
| 27 - Q3 | $150 | $12,016 | 35 - Q3 | $150 | $52,532 |
| 27 - Q4 | $150 | $12,641 | 35 - Q4 | $150 | $54,550 |
| 28 - Q1 | $150 | $13,282 | 36 - Q1 | $150 | $56,623 |
| 28 - Q2 | $150 | $13,941 | 36 - Q2 | $150 | $58,752 |
| 28 - Q3 | $150 | $14,617 | 36 - Q3 | $150 | $60,938 |
| 28 - Q4 | $150 | $15,312 | 36 - Q4 | $150 | $63,184 |

| Age - Quarter | Monthly | Balance | Age - Quarter | Monthly | Balance |
|---|---|---|---|---|---|
| 37 - Q1 | $150 | $65,490 | 46 - Q3 | $150 | $230,879 |
| 37 - Q2 | $150 | $67,858 | 46 - Q4 | $150 | $238,012 |
| 37 - Q3 | $150 | $70,290 | 47 - Q1 | $150 | $245,339 |
| 37 - Q4 | $150 | $72,788 | 47 - Q2 | $150 | $252,863 |
| 38 - Q1 | $150 | $75,353 | 47 - Q3 | $150 | $260,590 |
| 38 - Q2 | $150 | $77,988 | 47 - Q4 | $150 | $268,526 |
| 38 - Q3 | $150 | $80,694 | 48 - Q1 | $150 | $276,676 |
| 38 - Q4 | $150 | $83,472 | 48 - Q2 | $150 | $285,047 |
| 39 - Q1 | $150 | $86,326 | 48 - Q3 | $150 | $293,643 |
| 39 - Q2 | $150 | $89,257 | 48 - Q4 | $150 | $302,471 |
| 39 - Q3 | $150 | $92,267 | 49 - Q1 | $150 | $311,538 |
| 39 - Q4 | $150 | $95,358 | 49 - Q2 | $150 | $320,850 |
| 40 - Q1 | $150 | $98,833 | 49 - Q3 | $150 | $330,413 |
| 40 - Q2 | $150 | $102,401 | 49 - Q4 | $150 | $340,234 |
| 40 - Q3 | $150 | $106,066 | 50 - Q1 | $150 | $350,620 |
| 40 - Q4 | $150 | $109,830 | 50 - Q2 | $150 | $361,287 |
| 41 - Q1 | $150 | $113,695 | 50 - Q3 | $150 | $372,242 |
| 41 - Q2 | $150 | $117,665 | 50 - Q4 | $150 | $383,492 |
| 41 - Q3 | $150 | $121,742 | 51 - Q1 | $150 | $395,046 |
| 41 - Q4 | $150 | $125,929 | 51 - Q2 | $150 | $406,913 |
| 42 - Q1 | $150 | $130,229 | 51 - Q3 | $150 | $419,099 |
| 42 - Q2 | $150 | $134,645 | 51 - Q4 | $150 | $431,615 |
| 42 - Q3 | $150 | $139,181 | 52 - Q1 | $150 | $444,469 |
| 42 - Q4 | $150 | $143,839 | 52 - Q2 | $150 | $457,669 |
| 43 - Q1 | $150 | $148,623 | 52 - Q3 | $150 | $471,226 |
| 43 - Q2 | $150 | $153,535 | 52 - Q4 | $150 | $485,150 |
| 43 - Q3 | $150 | $158,581 | 53 - Q1 | $150 | $499,449 |
| 43 - Q4 | $150 | $163,762 | 53 - Q2 | $150 | $514,134 |
| 44 - Q1 | $150 | $169,084 | 53 - Q3 | $150 | $529,215 |
| 44 - Q2 | $150 | $174,549 | 53 - Q4 | $150 | $544,704 |
| 44 - Q3 | $150 | $180,162 | 54 - Q1 | $150 | $560,611 |
| 44 - Q4 | $150 | $185,927 | 54 - Q2 | $150 | $576,948 |
| 45 - Q1 | $150 | $191,847 | 54 - Q3 | $150 | $593,725 |
| 45 - Q2 | $150 | $197,927 | 54 - Q4 | $150 | $610,956 |
| 45 - Q3 | $150 | $204,171 | 55 - Q1 | $150 | $628,652 |
| 45 - Q4 | $150 | $210,583 | 55 - Q2 | $150 | $646,825 |
| 46 - Q1 | $150 | $217,169 | 55 - Q3 | $150 | $665,490 |
| 46 - Q2 | $150 | $223,932 | 55 - Q4 | $150 | $684,658 |

| Age - Quarter | Monthly | Balance | Age - Quarter | Monthly | Balance |
|---|---|---|---|---|---|
| 56 - Q1 | $150 | $704,344 | 61 - Q1 | $150 | $1,231,312 |
| 56 - Q2 | $150 | $724,561 | 61 - Q2 | $150 | $1,265,758 |
| 56 - Q3 | $150 | $745,324 | 61 - Q3 | $150 | $1,301,133 |
| 56 - Q4 | $150 | $766,648 | 61 - Q4 | $150 | $1,337,464 |
| 57 - Q1 | $150 | $788,547 | 62 - Q1 | $150 | $1,374,775 |
| 57 - Q2 | $150 | $811,038 | 62 - Q2 | $150 | $1,413,094 |
| 57 - Q3 | $150 | $834,136 | 62 - Q3 | $150 | $1,452,448 |
| 57 - Q4 | $150 | $857,858 | 62 - Q4 | $150 | $1,492,864 |
| 58 - Q1 | $150 | $882,220 | 63 - Q1 | $150 | $1,534,371 |
| 58 - Q2 | $150 | $907,240 | 63 - Q2 | $150 | $1,576,999 |
| 58 - Q3 | $150 | $932,935 | 63 - Q3 | $150 | $1,620,778 |
| 58 - Q4 | $150 | $959,325 | 63 - Q4 | $150 | $1,665,739 |
| 59 - Q1 | $150 | $986,427 | 64 - Q1 | $150 | $1,711,914 |
| 59 - Q2 | $150 | $1,014,260 | 64 - Q2 | $150 | $1,759,336 |
| 59 - Q3 | $150 | $1,042,845 | 64 - Q3 | $150 | $1,808,038 |
| 59 - Q4 | $150 | $1,072,202 | 64 - Q4 | $150 | $1,858,055 |
| 60 - Q1 | $150 | $1,102,351 | 65 - Q1 | $150 | $1,909,423 |
| 60 - Q2 | $150 | $1,133,315 | 65 - Q2 | $150 | $1,962,177 |
| 60 - Q3 | $150 | $1,165,114 | 65 - Q3 | $150 | $2,016,356 |
| 60 - Q4 | $150 | $1,197,772 | 65 - Q4 | $150 | $2,071,998 |

# APPENDIX B – INVESTMENT COMPANIES AND THEIR INDEX FUNDS

## 1) Charles Schwab – www.schwab.com

Large Cap Index Funds:
SWPPX – Schwab S&P 500
SWTSX – Schwab Total Stock Market

Small Cap Index Fund:
SWSSX – Schwab Small Cap

International Index Fund:
SWISX – Schwab International

## 2) Fidelity – www.fidelity.com

Large Cap Index Funds:
FSTMX – Spartan Total Market
FUSEX – Spartan 500 Index

Small Cap Index Fund:
FSSPX – Spartan Small Cap

International Index Fund:
FSIIX – Spartan International

3) **Vanguard – www.vanguard.com**

Large Cap Index Funds:
VFINX – Vanguard 500
VTSMX – Vanguard Total Stock Market

Small Cap Index Fund:
NAESX – Vanguard Small Cap

International Index Fund:
VGTSX – Vanguard Total International Stock

4) **T. Rowe Price – www.troweprice.com**

Large Cap Index Funds:
PREIX – T. Rowe Price Equity Index 500
POMIX – T. Rowe Price Total Equity Market

Small Cap Index Fund:
N/A

International Index Fund:
PIEQX – T. Rowe Price International Equity

5) **Thrift Savings Plan (TSP) – Federal Employees**

Large Cap Index Fund:
C Fund – S&P 500

Small Cap Index Fund:
S Fund – Small-to-Mid Cap

International Index Fund:
I Fund – International

Special considerations:

1) Some of the companies above offer special classes of index funds (that have slightly lower fees) for accounts that have a minimum of $10,000 invested.

2) Each investment company requires a different amount in terms of initial investment and also subsequent (monthly) investments. Minimum initial investment amounts can range from $1 - $5,000 depending on the company. Also, minimum subsequent investments can range from $1 to $500.

# APPENDIX C – RECOMMENDED BOOKS

1) The Total Money Makeover – Dave Ramsey

2) The Millionaire Next Door – Thomas J. Stanley

3) The Automatic Millionaire – David Bach

4) Rich Dad, Poor Dad – Robert Kiyosaki

5) The Little Book of Common Sense Investing – John C. "Jack" Bogle

# ABOUT THE AUTHOR

M. Russell Giveans, PhD was born and raised in New Orleans, LA where he received his Bachelor of Science degree from Tulane University. He then went on to receive his PhD from the University of Minnesota in Minneapolis, MN. He currently resides in the Minneapolis area with his wife and children.

Dr. Giveans is dedicated to enhancing his life and the lives of those around him through wisdom and knowledge. He has served as a mentor and financial coach for many young people in their teens and twenties through his church and other local organizations. With so few people in today's culture having a solid understanding of investing and personal finance, he has used his own experiences and education from the past decade to develop a clear and concise road map to financial freedom. His goal with this book is to help people of all ages and income levels achieve success with their finances, and in their pursuit of long-term wealth accumulation.

Made in the USA
Monee, IL
29 November 2021

83375178R00085